LIBRO DE COLOREAR PARA ADULTOS
MANDALAS GEOMÉTRICAS

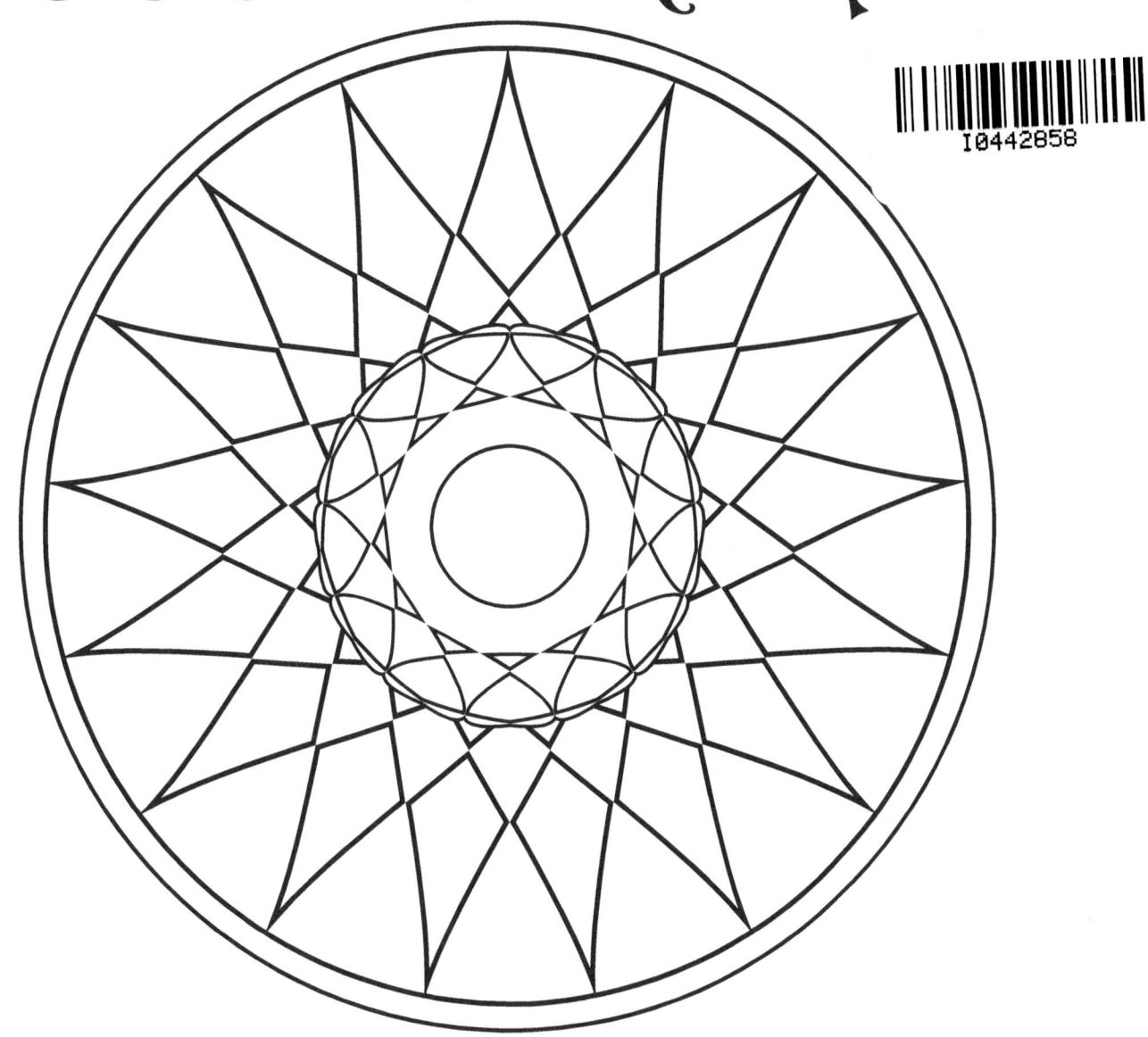

Relájate coloreando mandalas

MODERN STUDIO

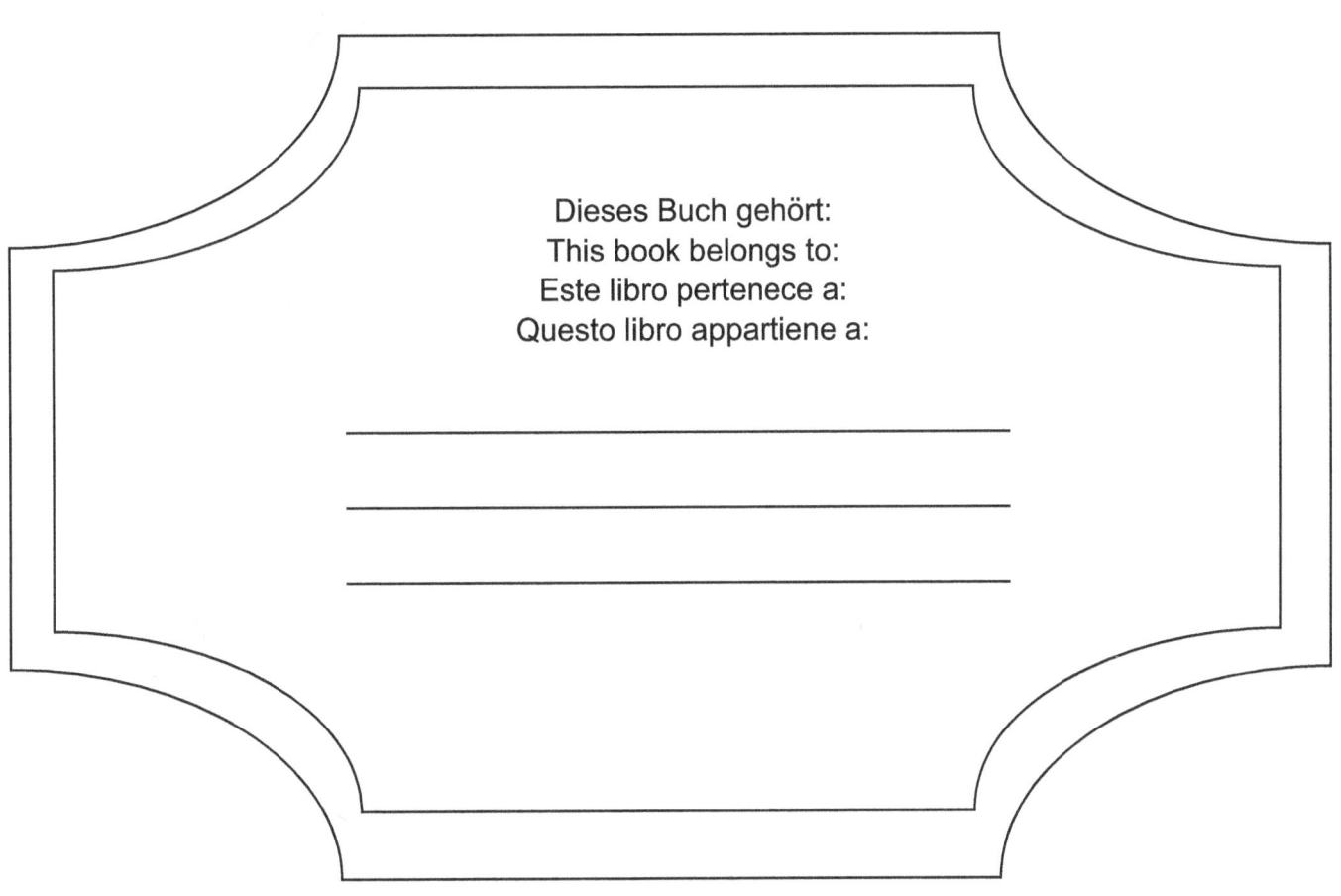

Folgen Sie Modern Studio auf Amazon.
Follow Modern Studio on Amazon.
Sigue a Modern Studio en Amazon.
Segui Modern Studio su Amazon.

https://www.amazon.com/Modern-Studio/e/B0887KDQYG

Instagram, Facebook.

Um über neue Bücher informiert zu werden, senden Sie eine E-Mail an:
To be updated on new books send an email to:
Para estar informado sobre nuevos libros envíe un correo electrónico a:
Per essere aggiornato su nuovi libri invia una mail a:

modernstudio.amazon@gmail.com

© **Copyright 2020 - All rights reserved.**
The content contained within this book may not be reproduced, duplicated or transmitted without direct written permission from the author or the publisher.

Under no circumstances will any blame or legal responsibility be held against the publisher, or author, for any damages, reparation, or monetary loss due to the information contained within this book, either directly or indirectly.

Legal Notice:
This book is copyright protected. It is only for personal use. You cannot amend, distribute, sell, use, quote or paraphrase any part, or the content within this book, without the consent of the author or publisher.

Disclaimer Notice:
Please note the information contained within this document is for educational and entertainment purposes only. All effort has been executed to present accurate, up to date, reliable, complete information. No warranties of any kind are declared or implied. Readers acknowledge that the author is not engaged in the rendering of legal, financial, medical or professional advice. The content within this book has been derived from various sources. Please consult a licensed professional before attempting any techniques outlined in this book.

By reading this document, the reader agrees that under no circumstances is the author responsible for any losses, direct or indirect, that are incurred as a result of the use of the information contained within this document, including, but not limited to, errors, omissions, or inaccuracies.

Es wird empfohlen, Bleistift- oder Wachsfarben zu verwenden.
It is recommended to use pencil or wax colors.
Si recomienda usar colores de lápiz o cera.
È consigliato usare colori a matita o a cera.

TEST

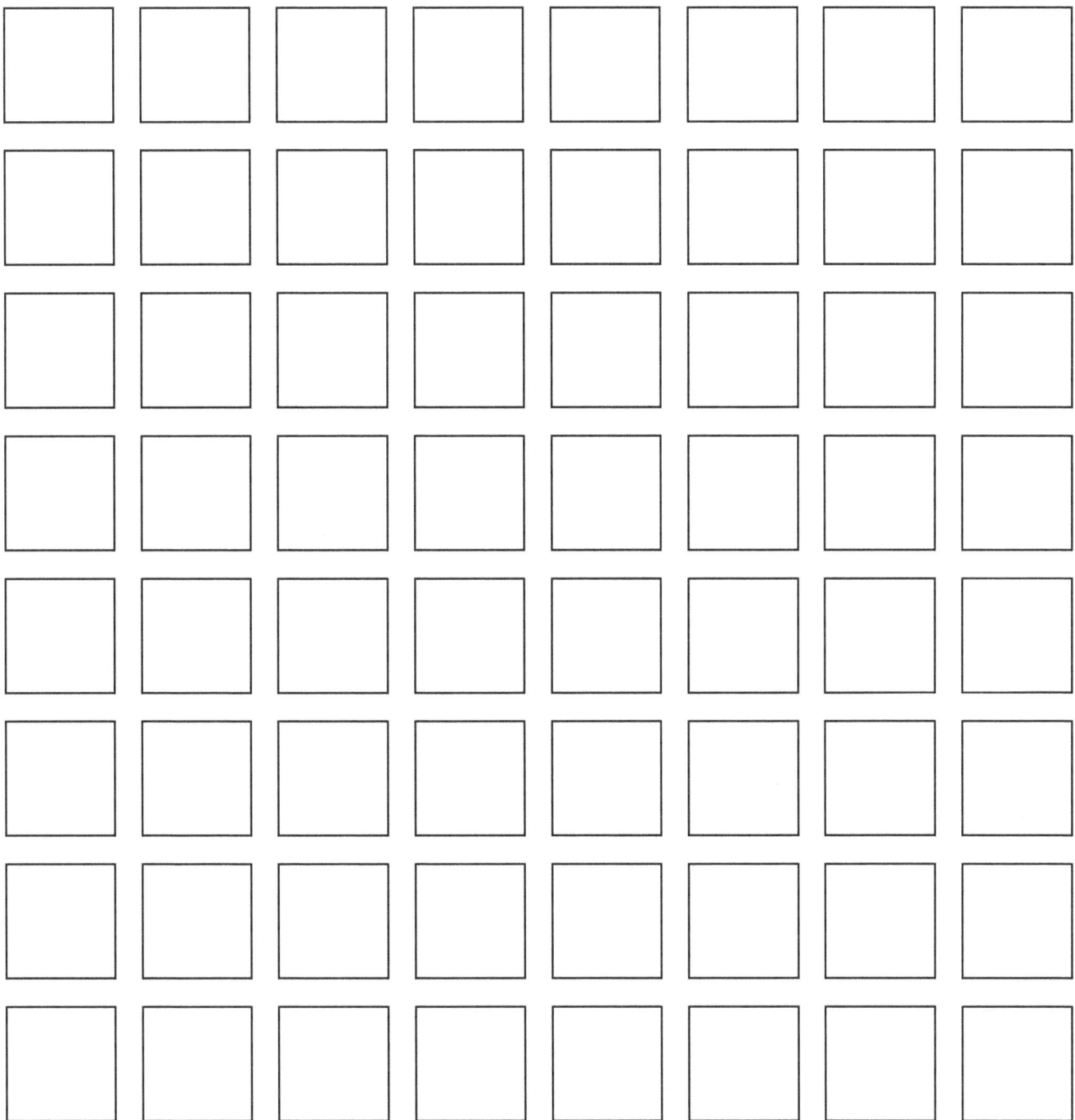

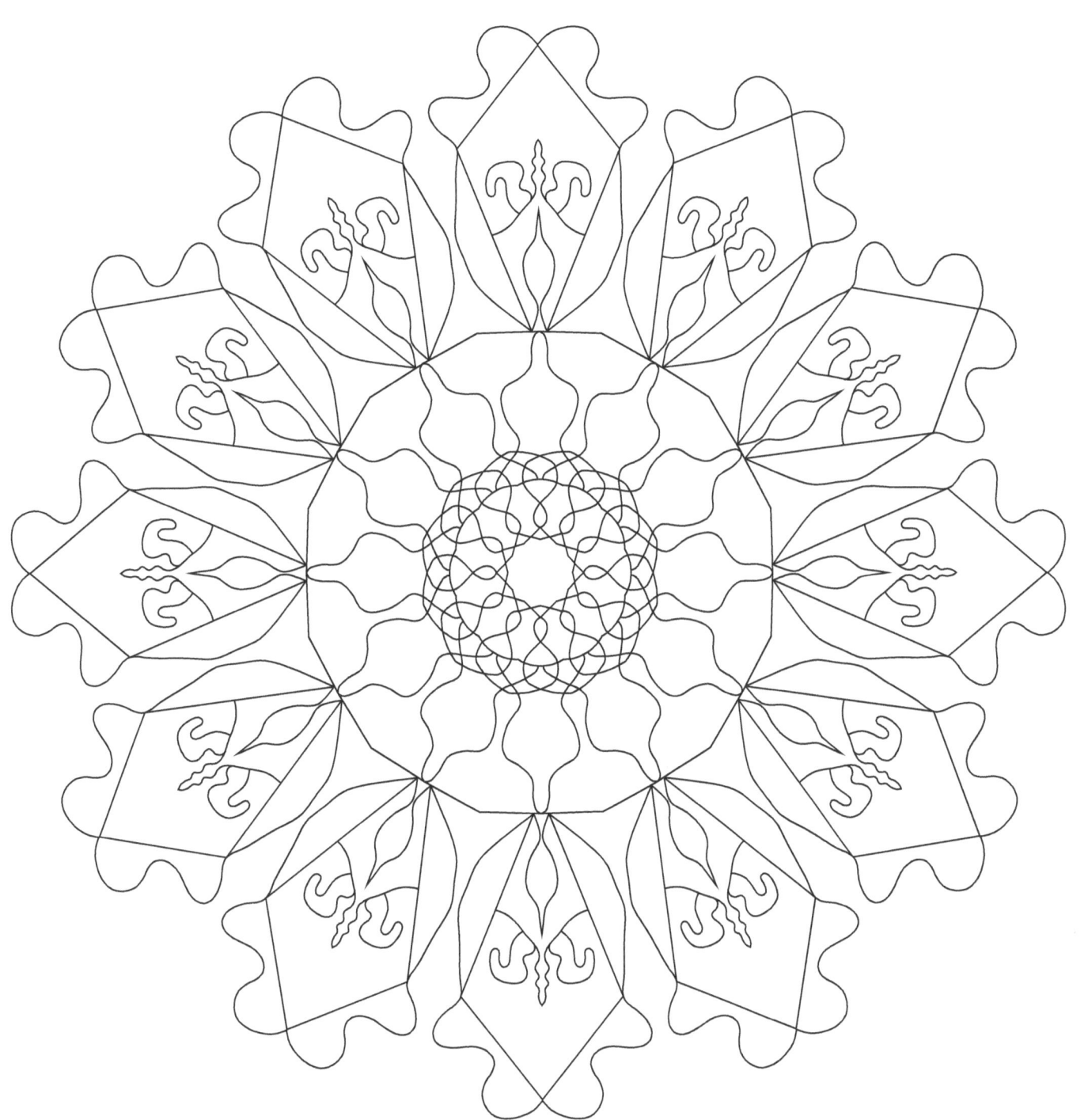

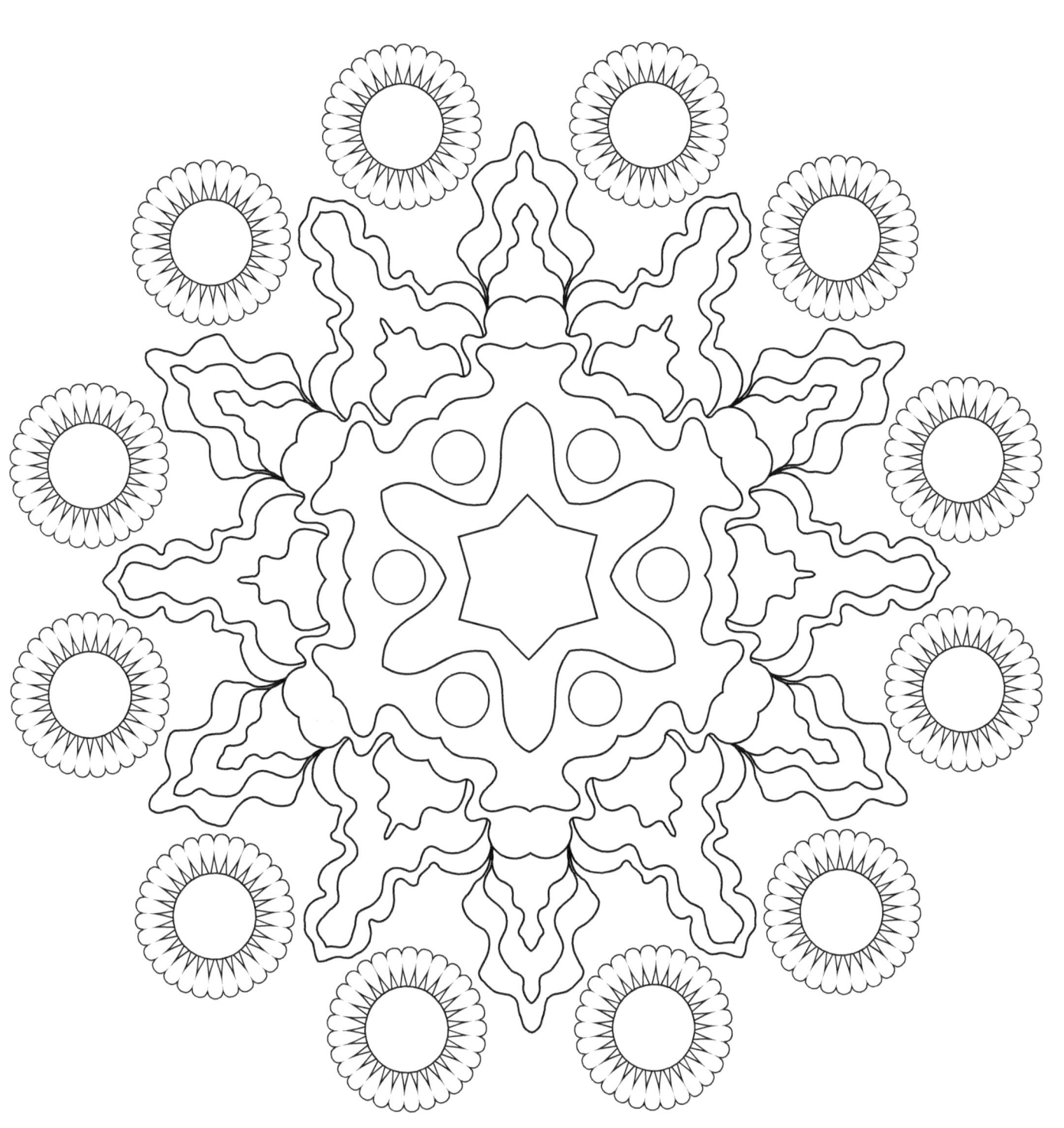

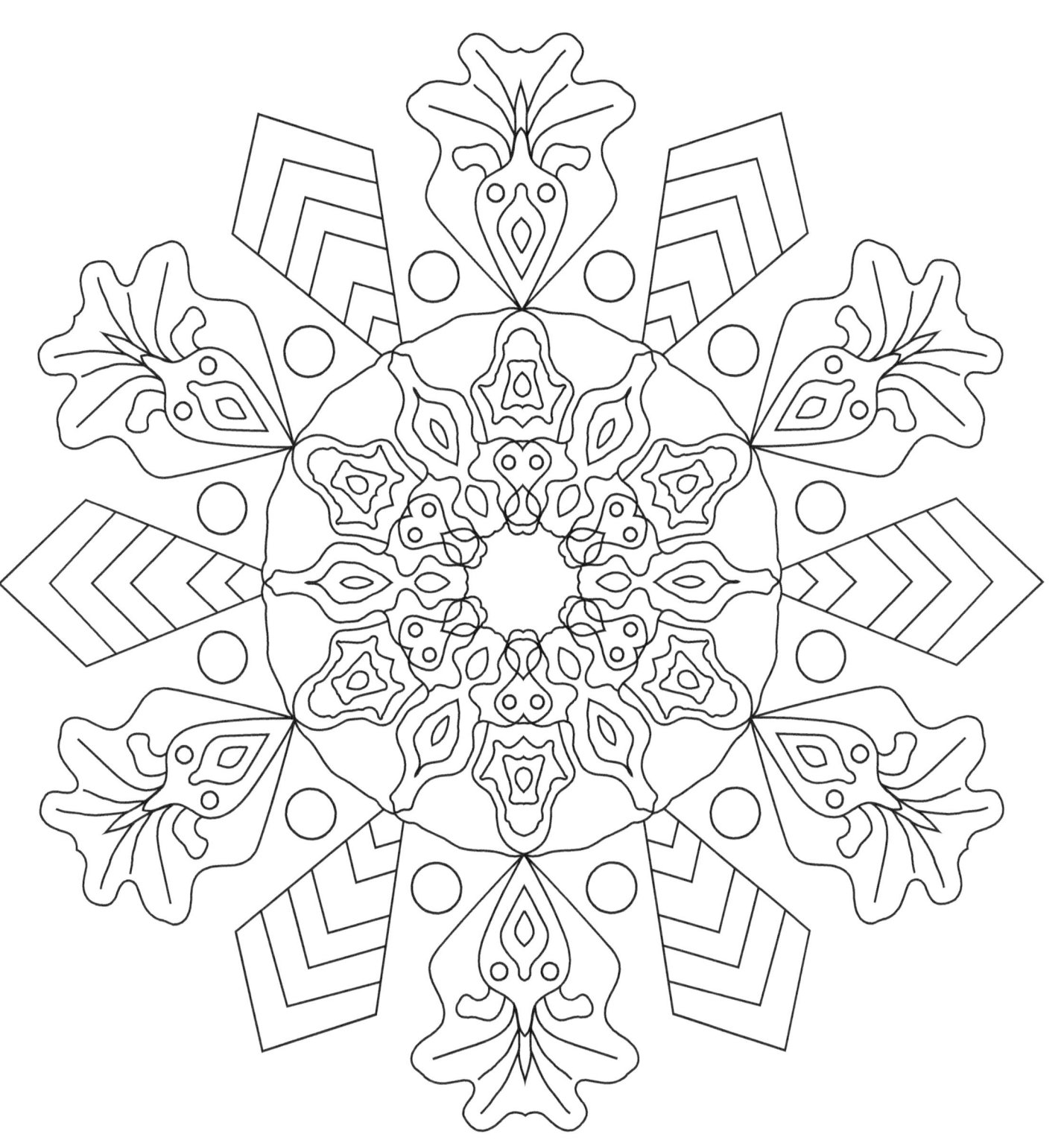

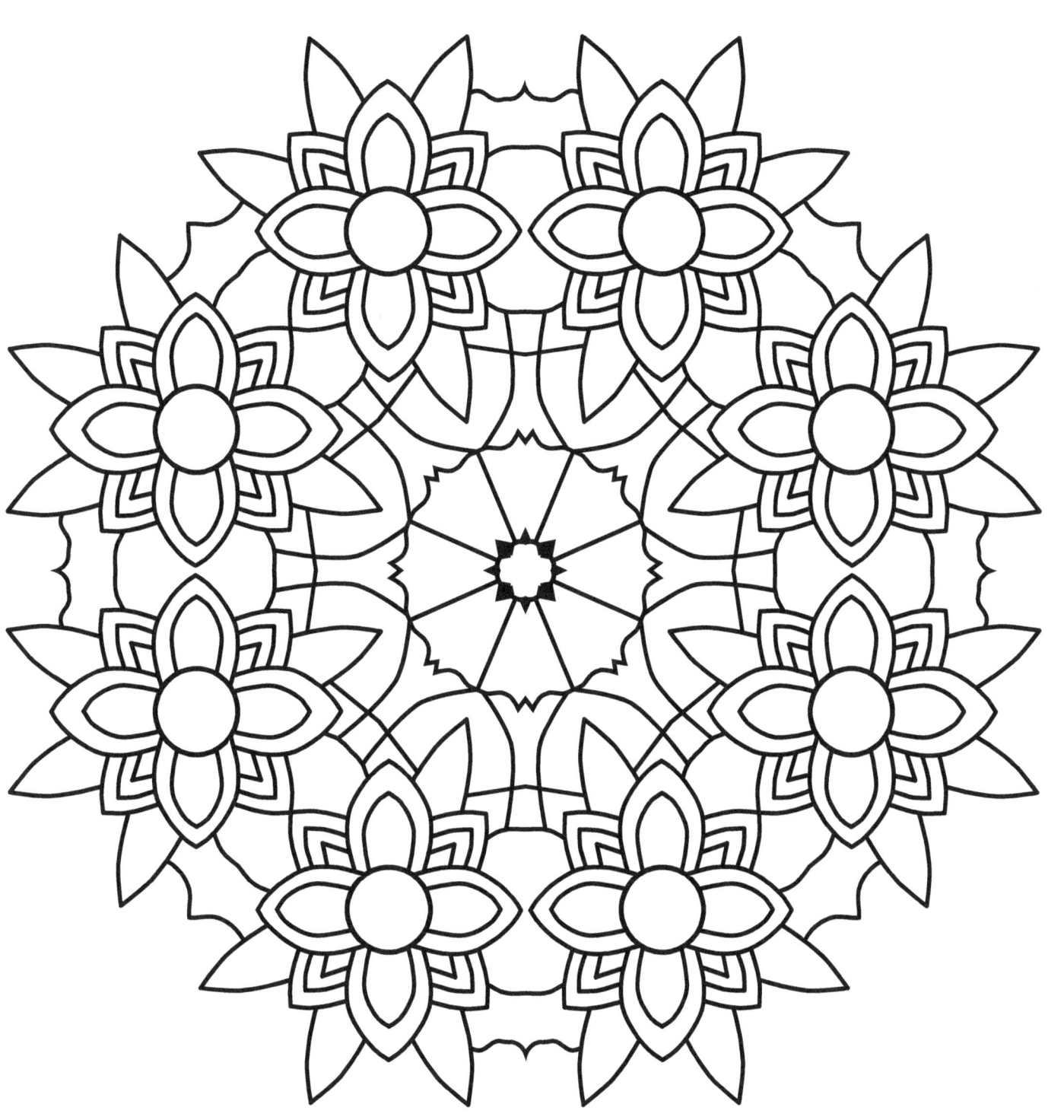

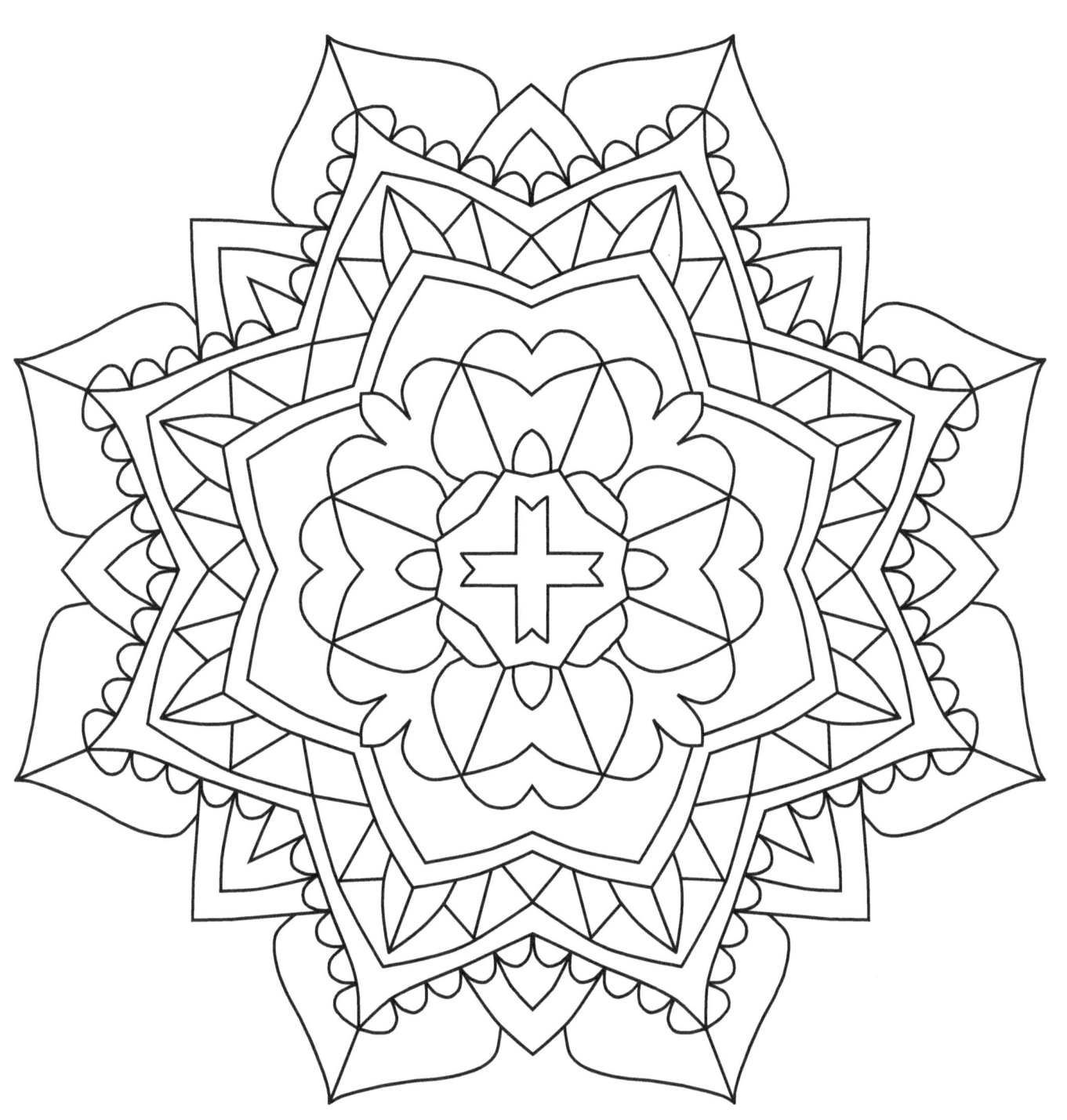

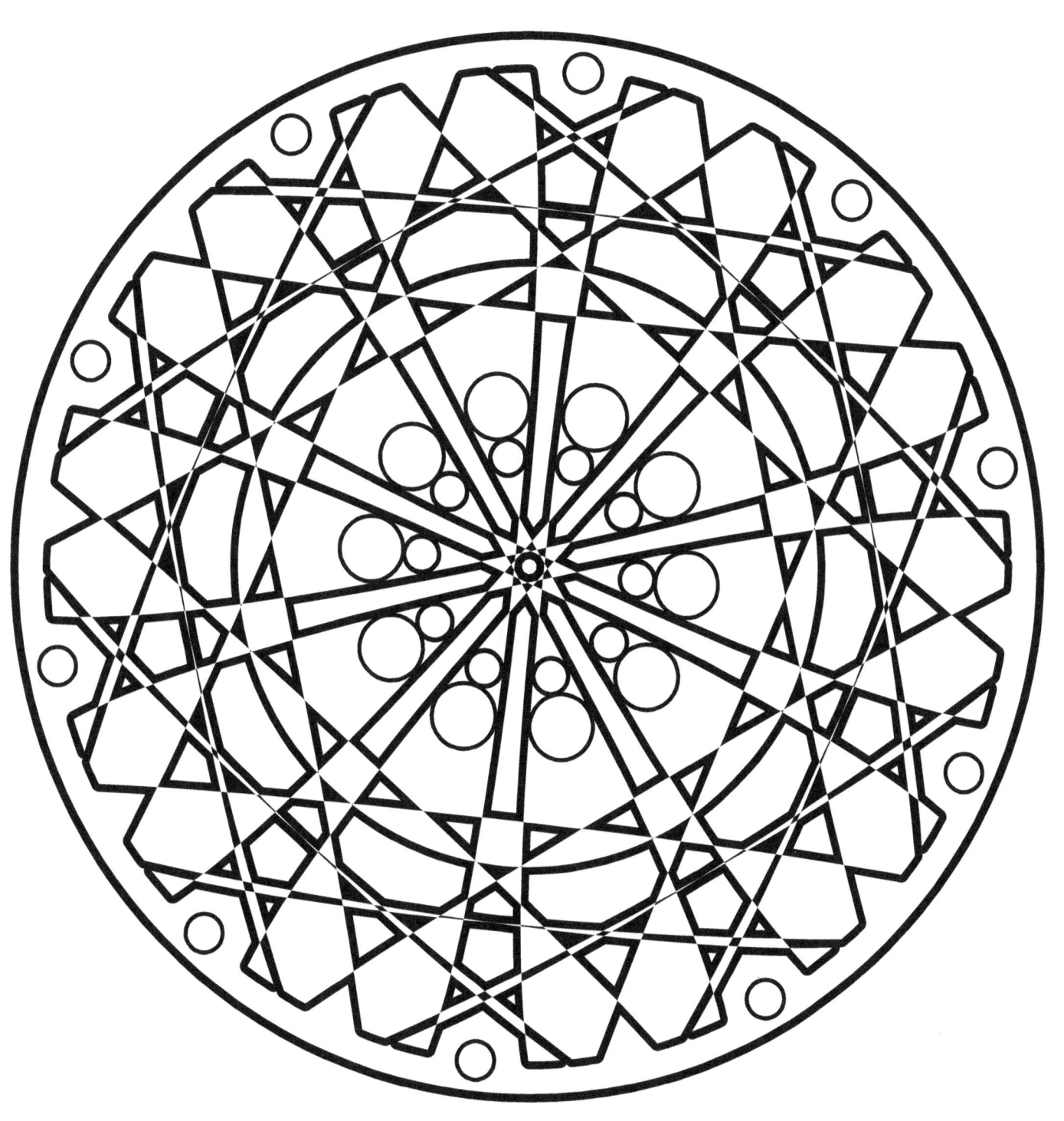

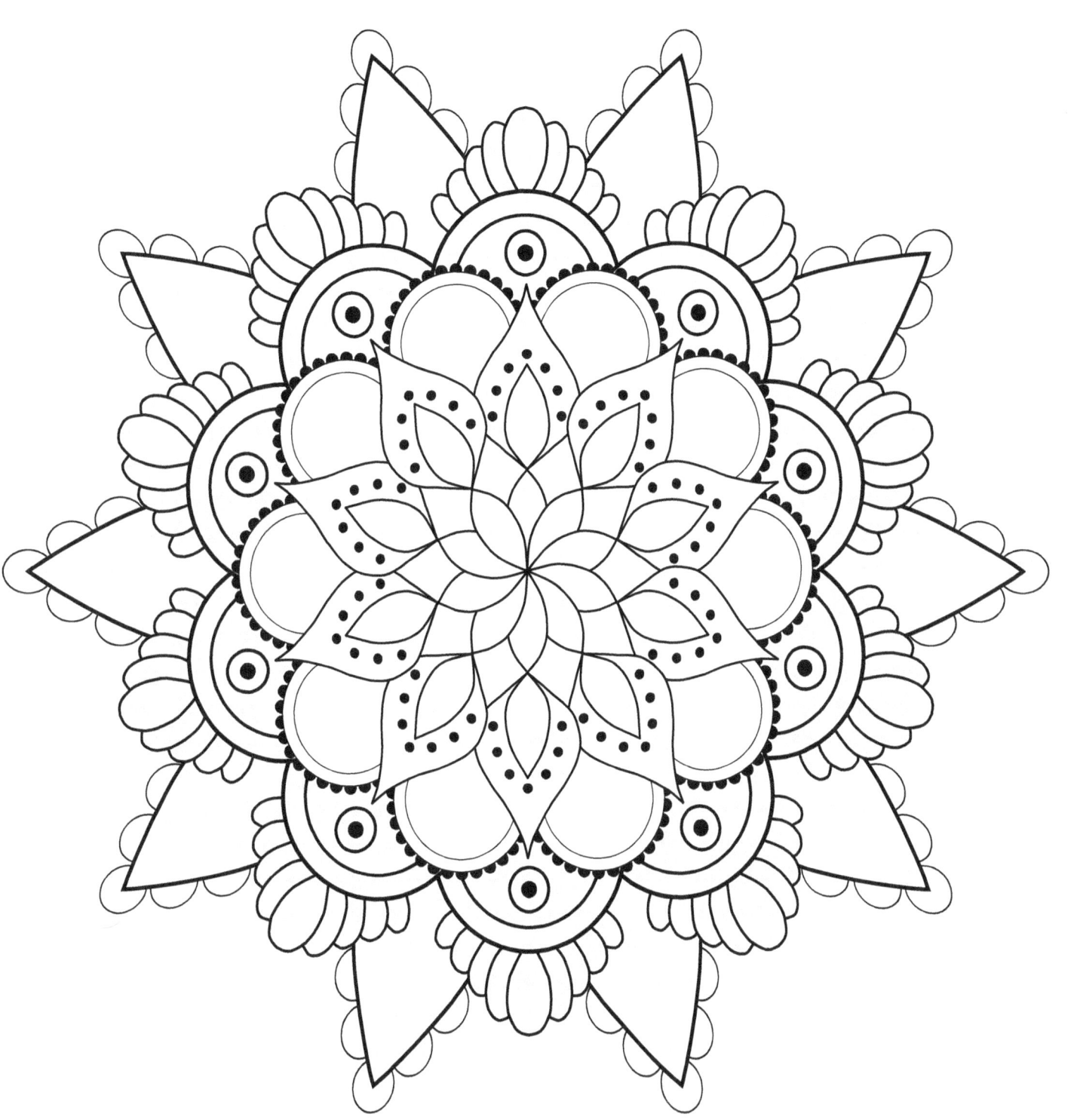

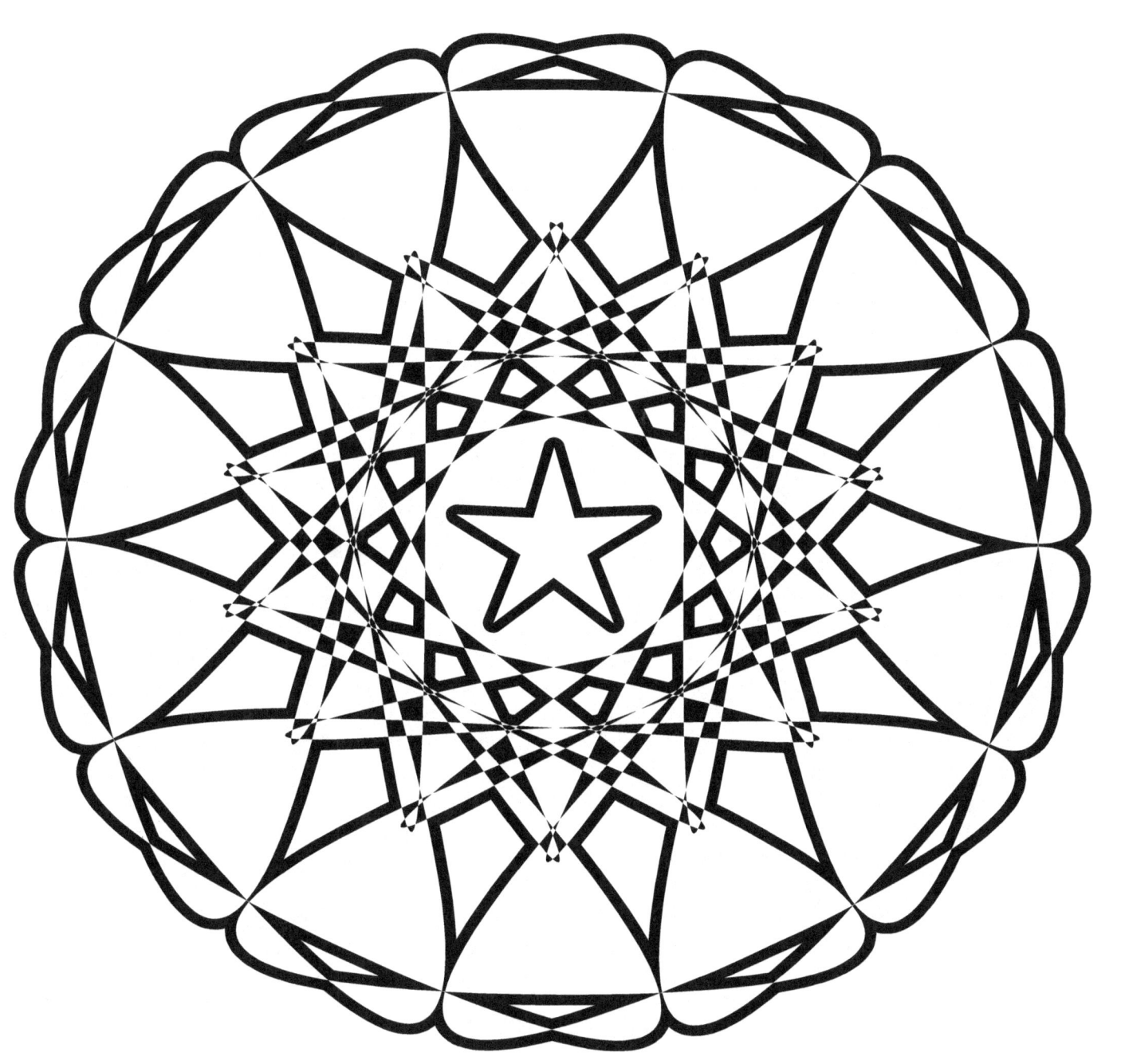

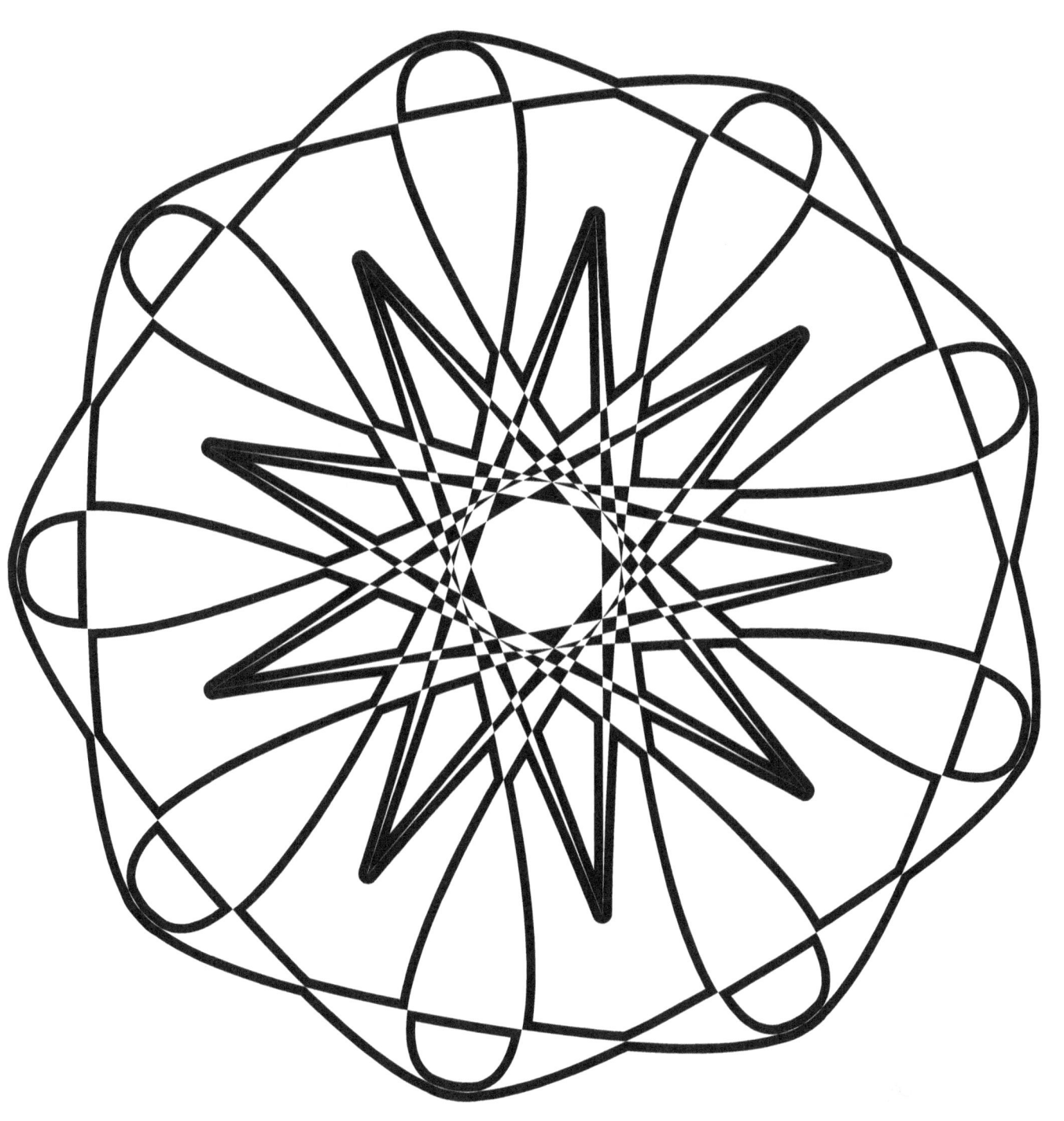

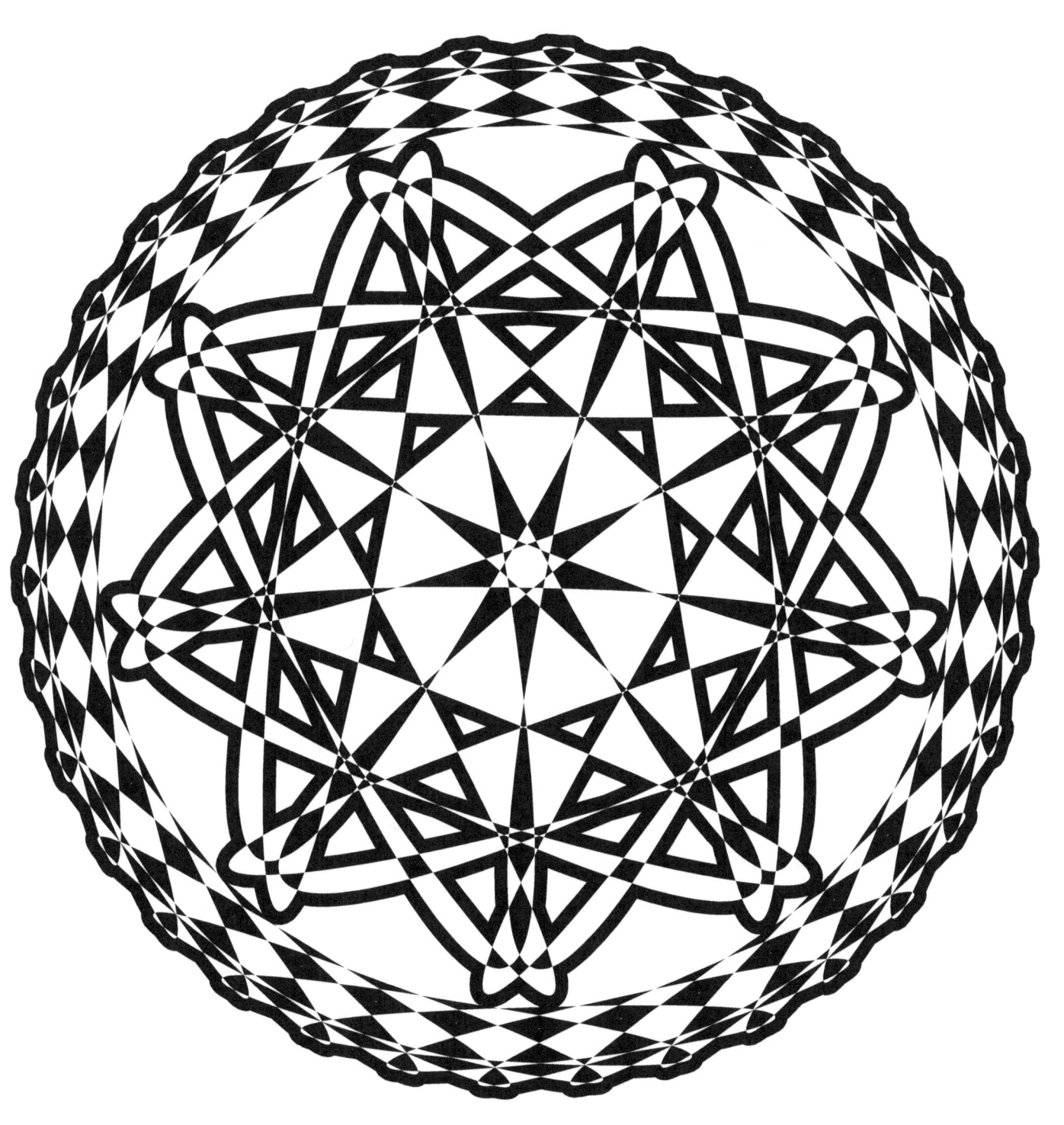

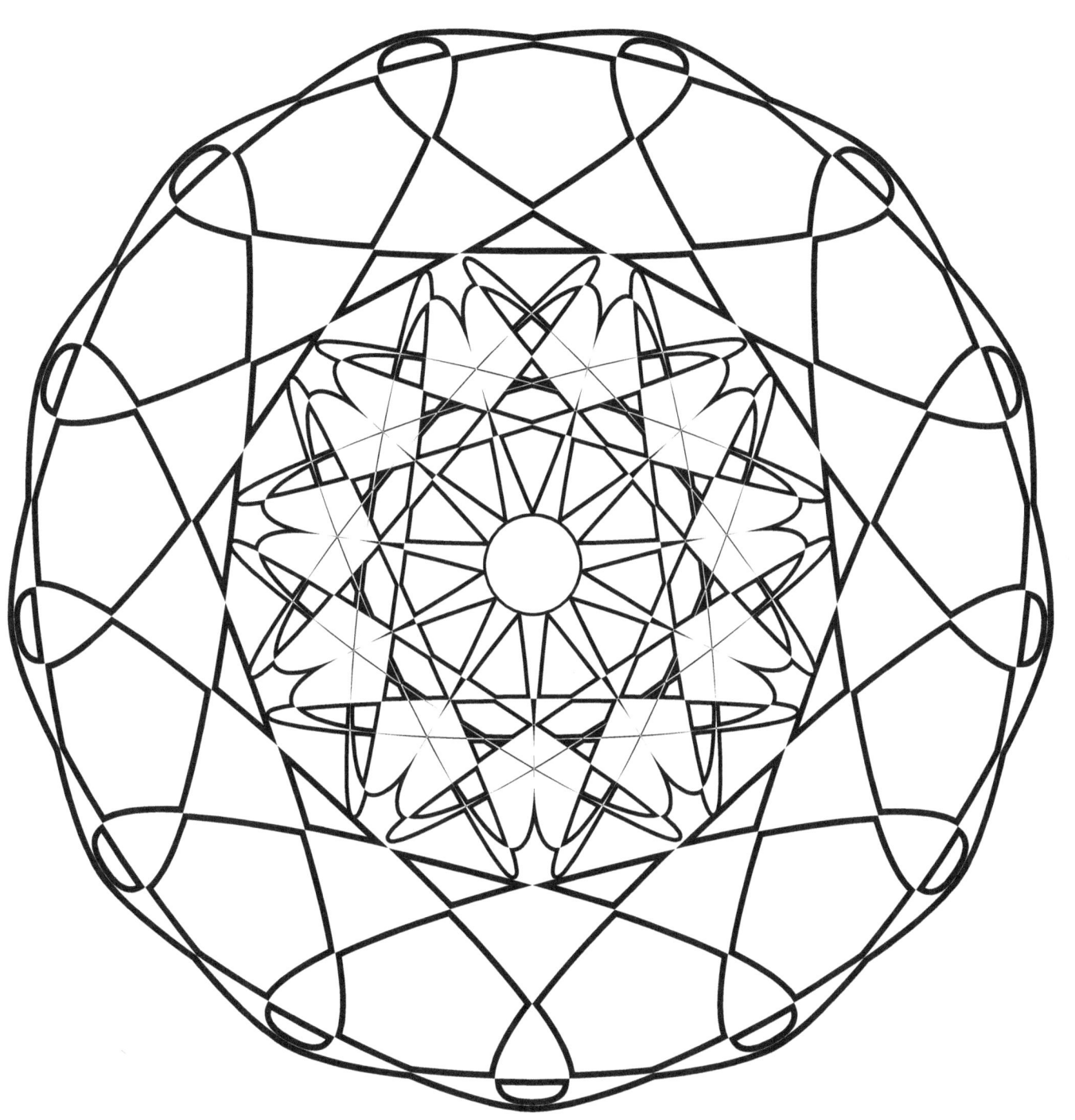

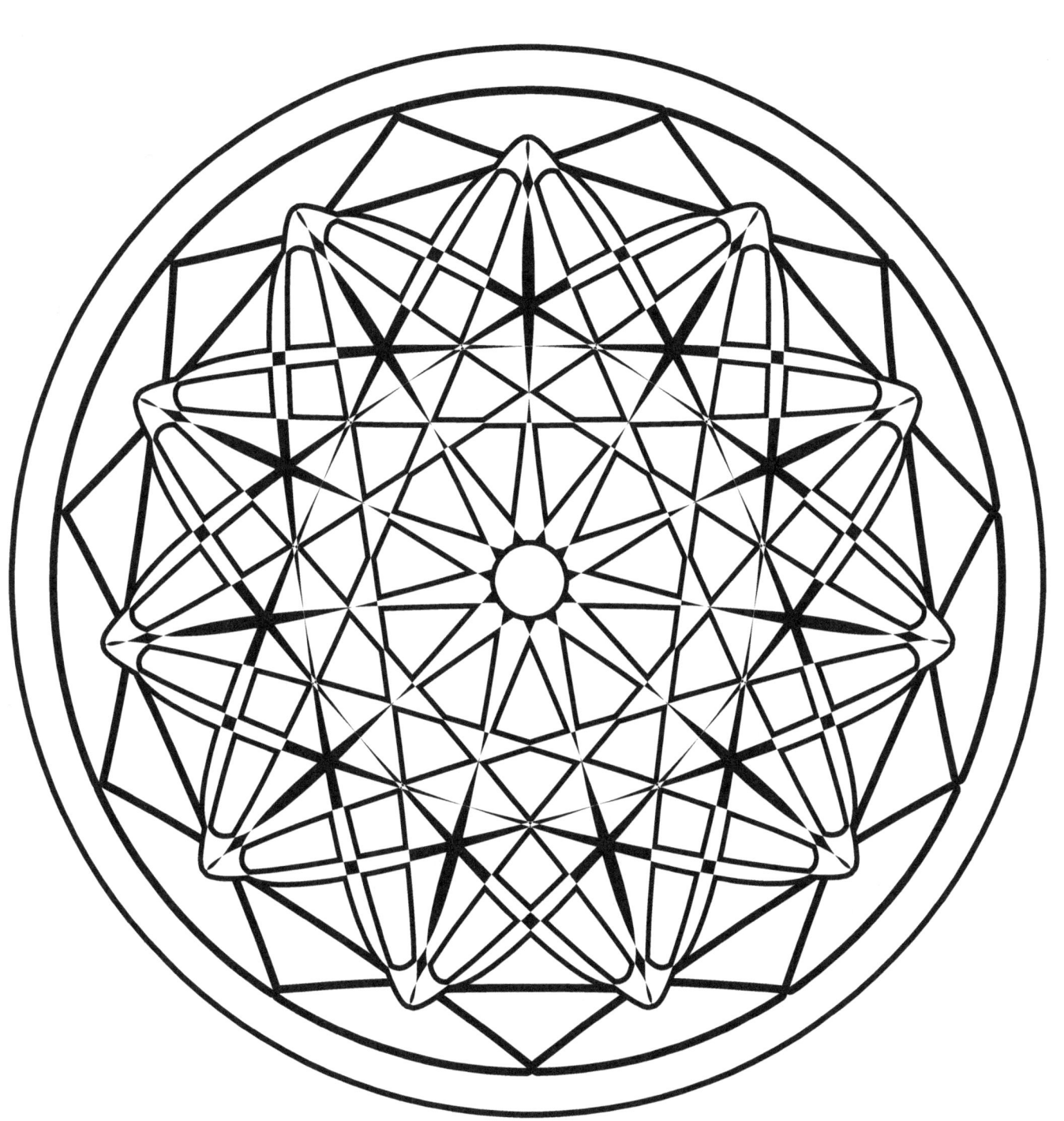

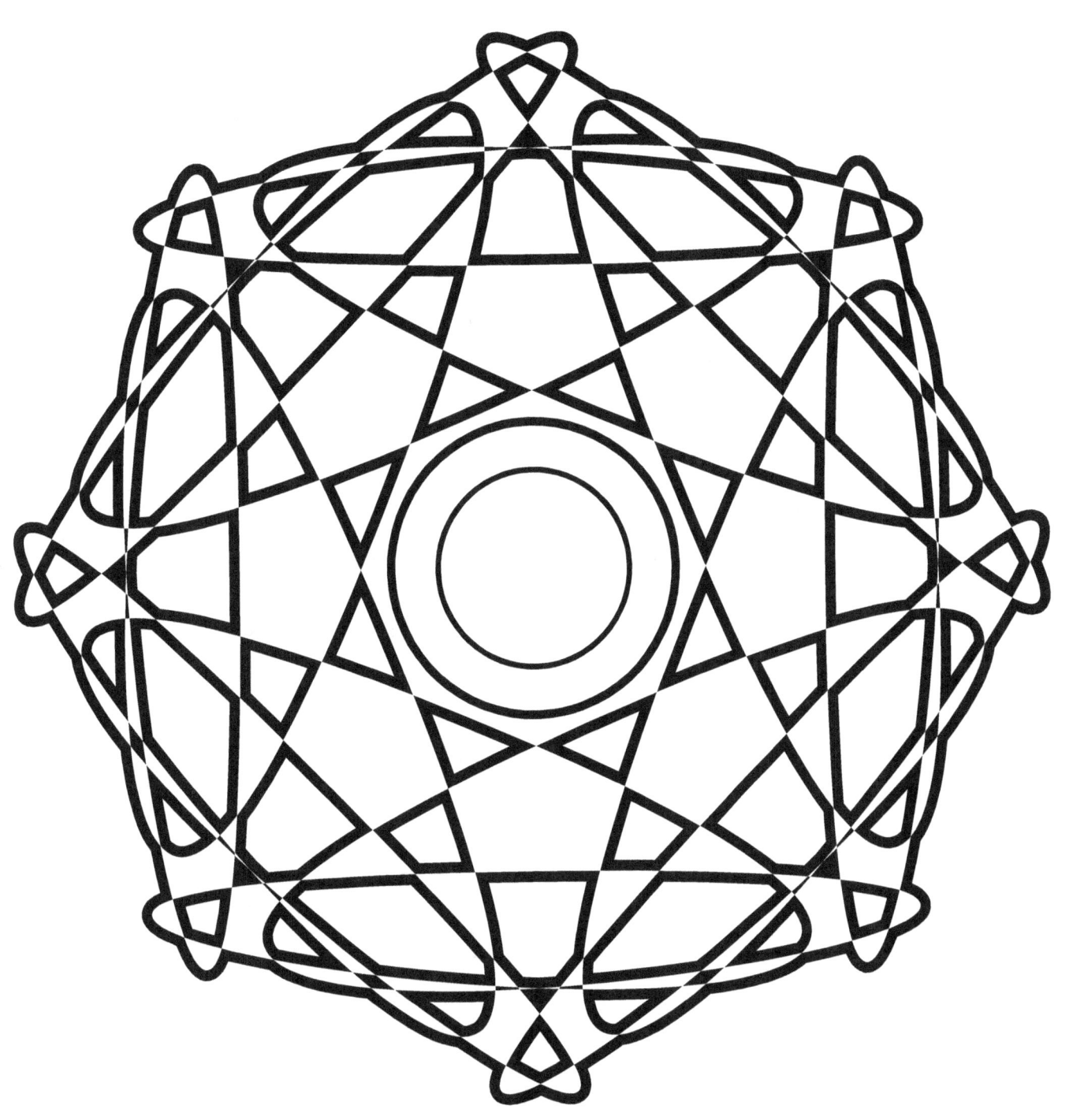

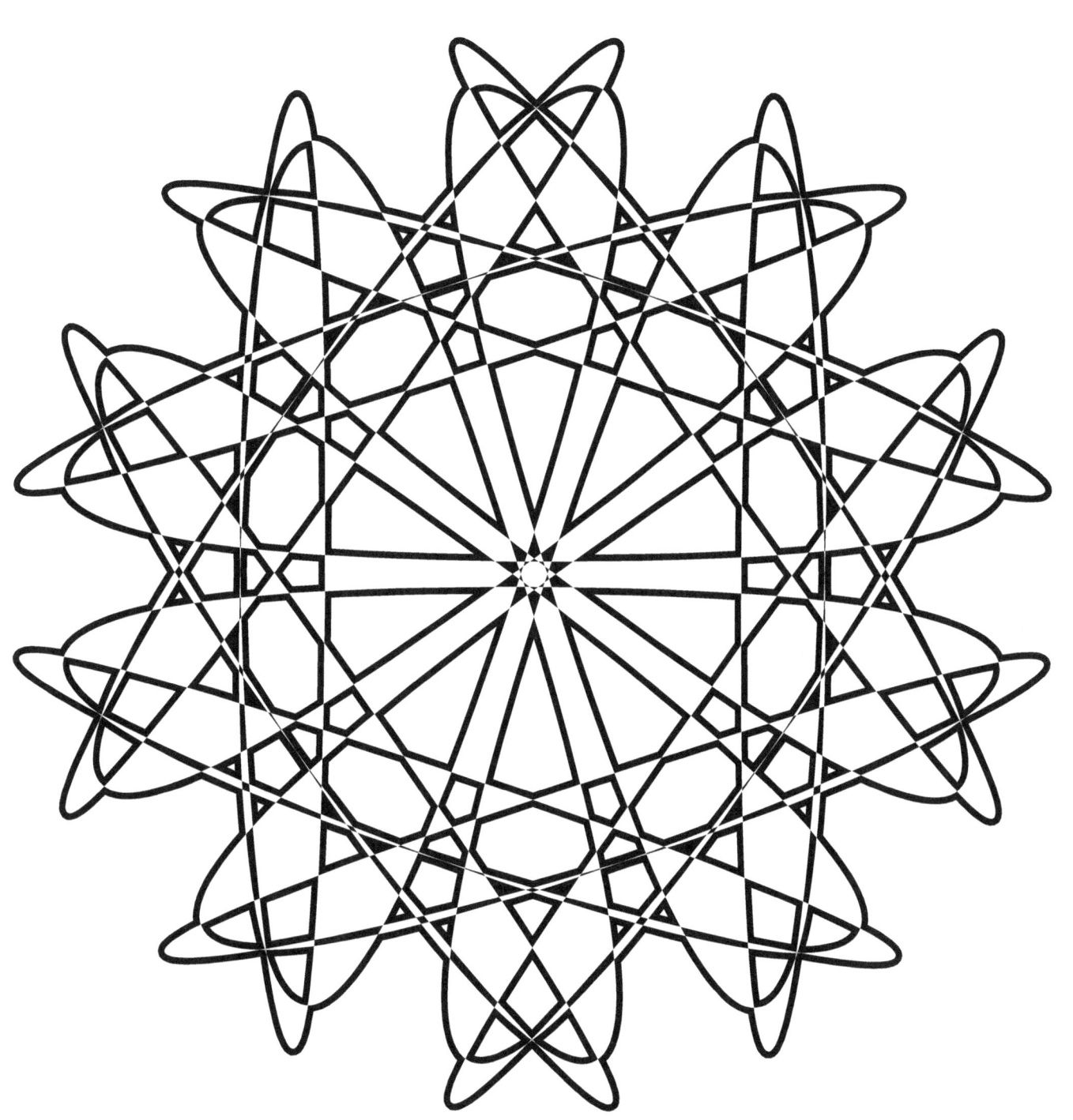

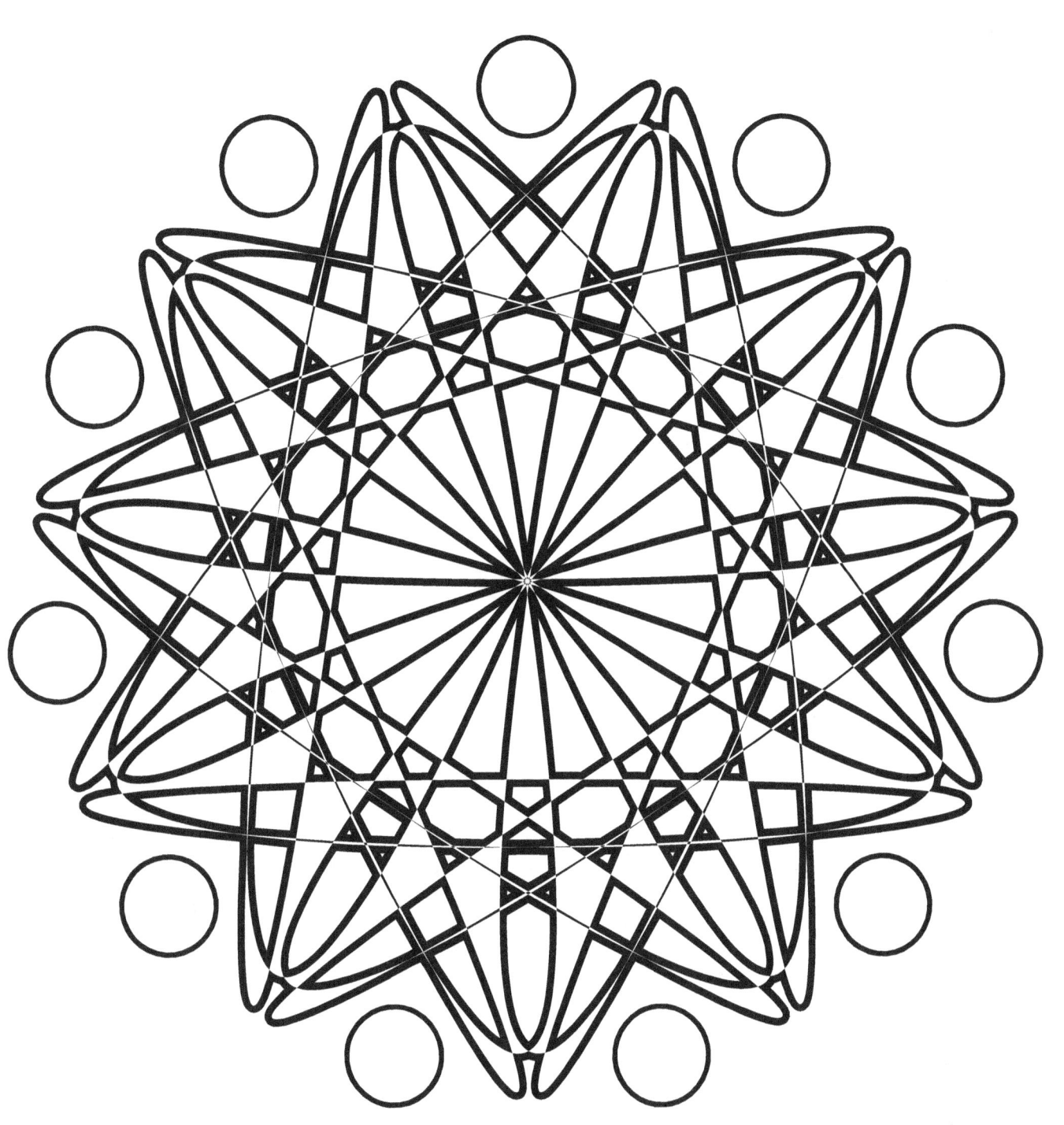

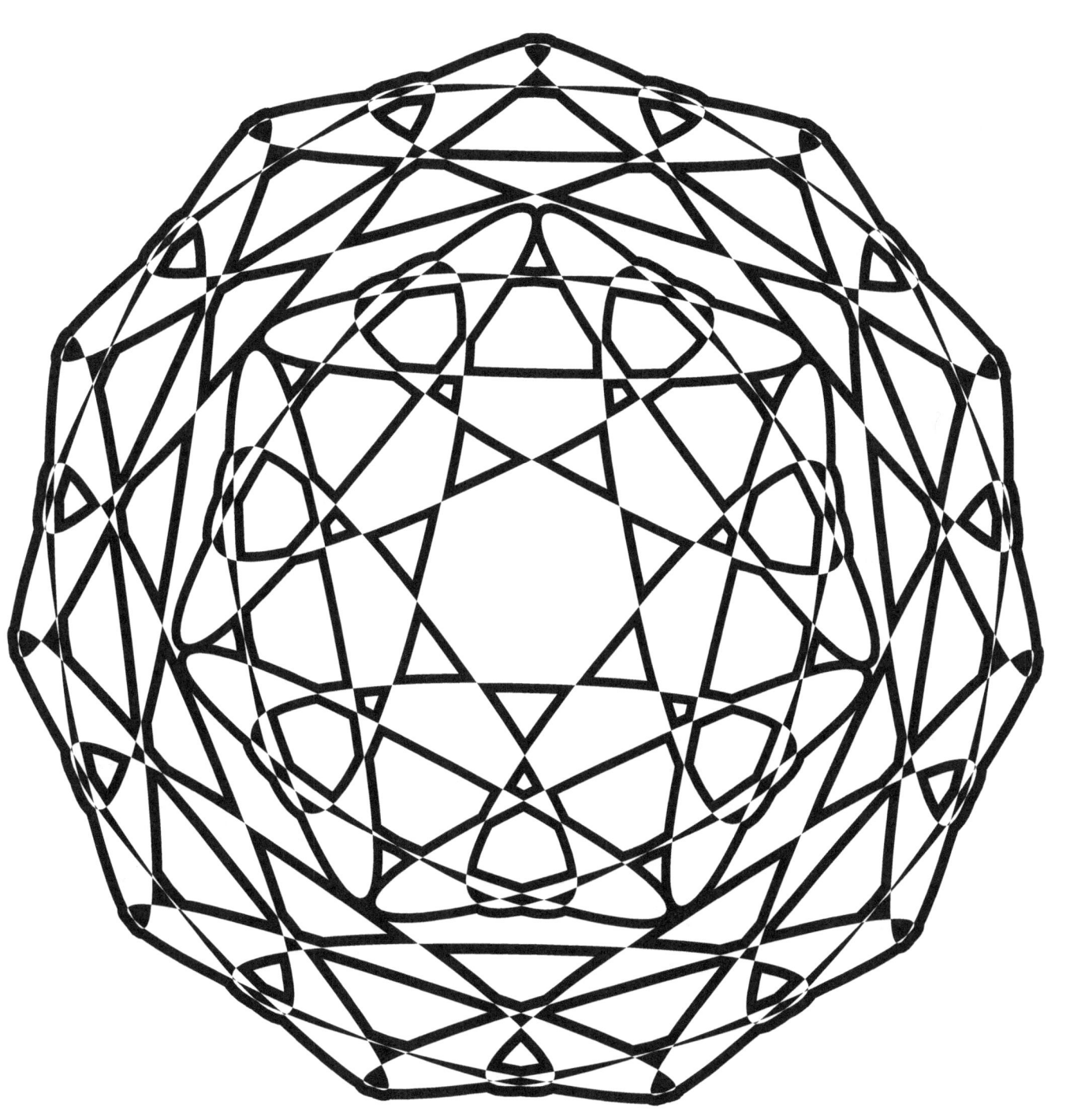

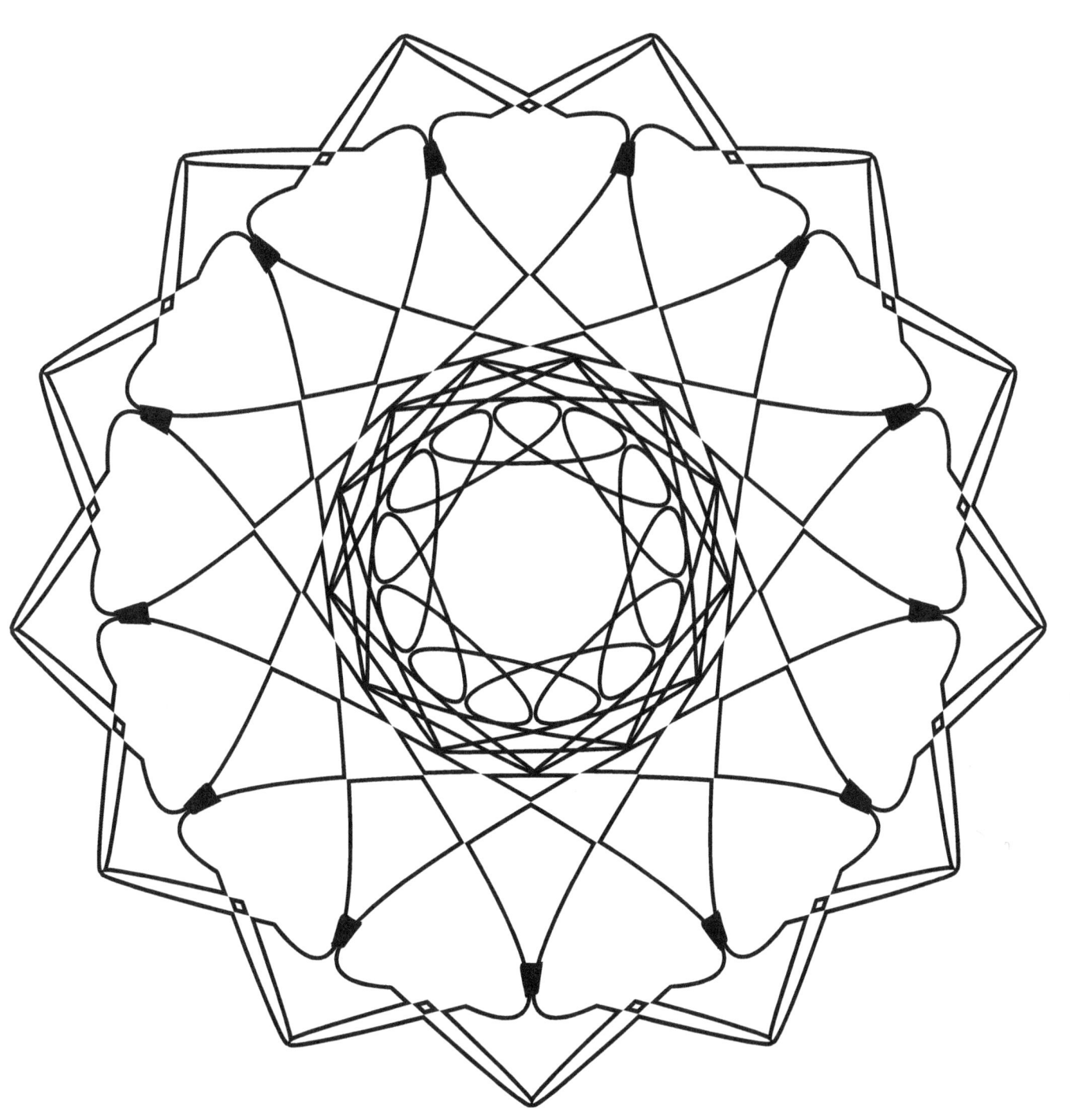

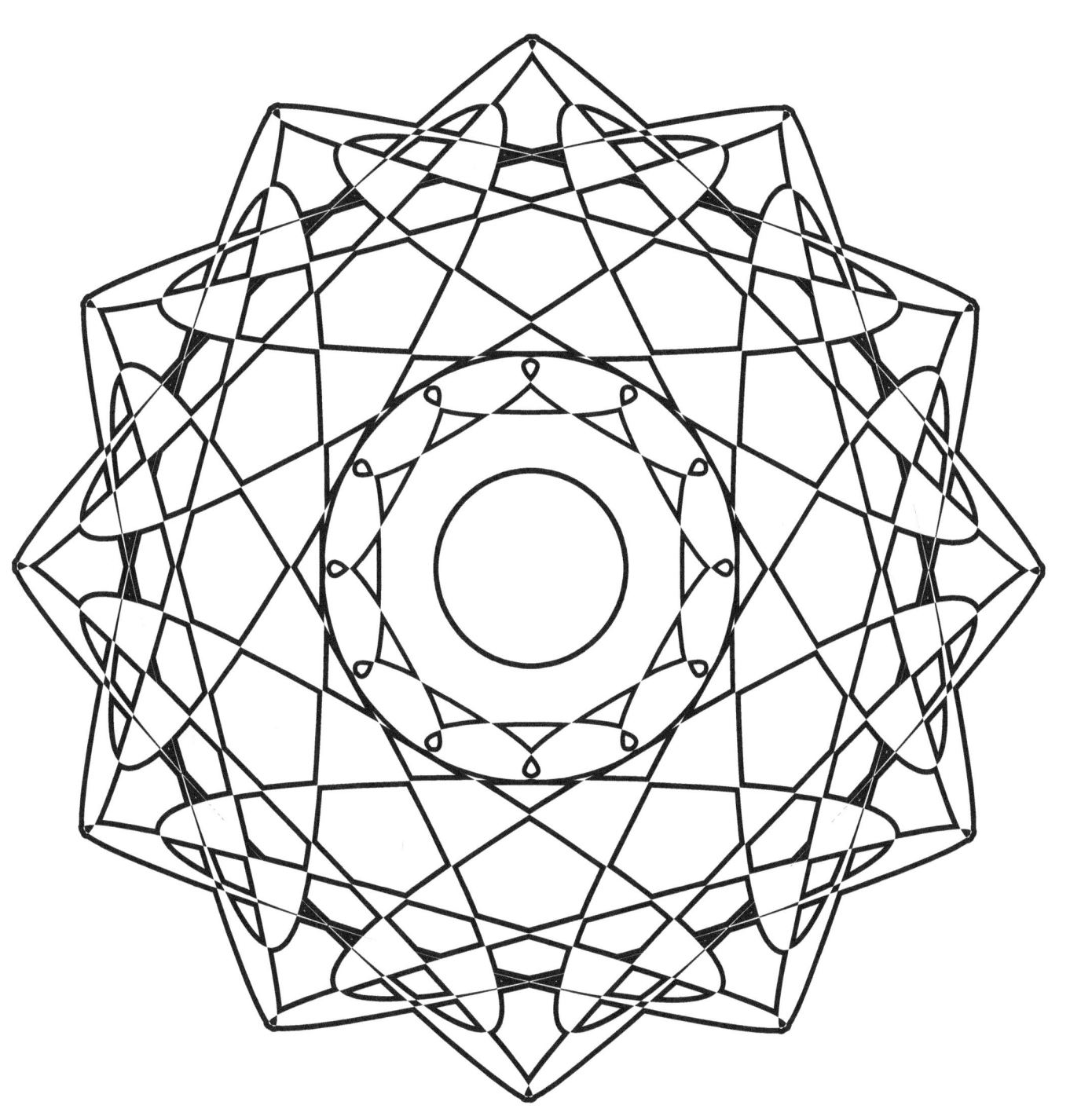

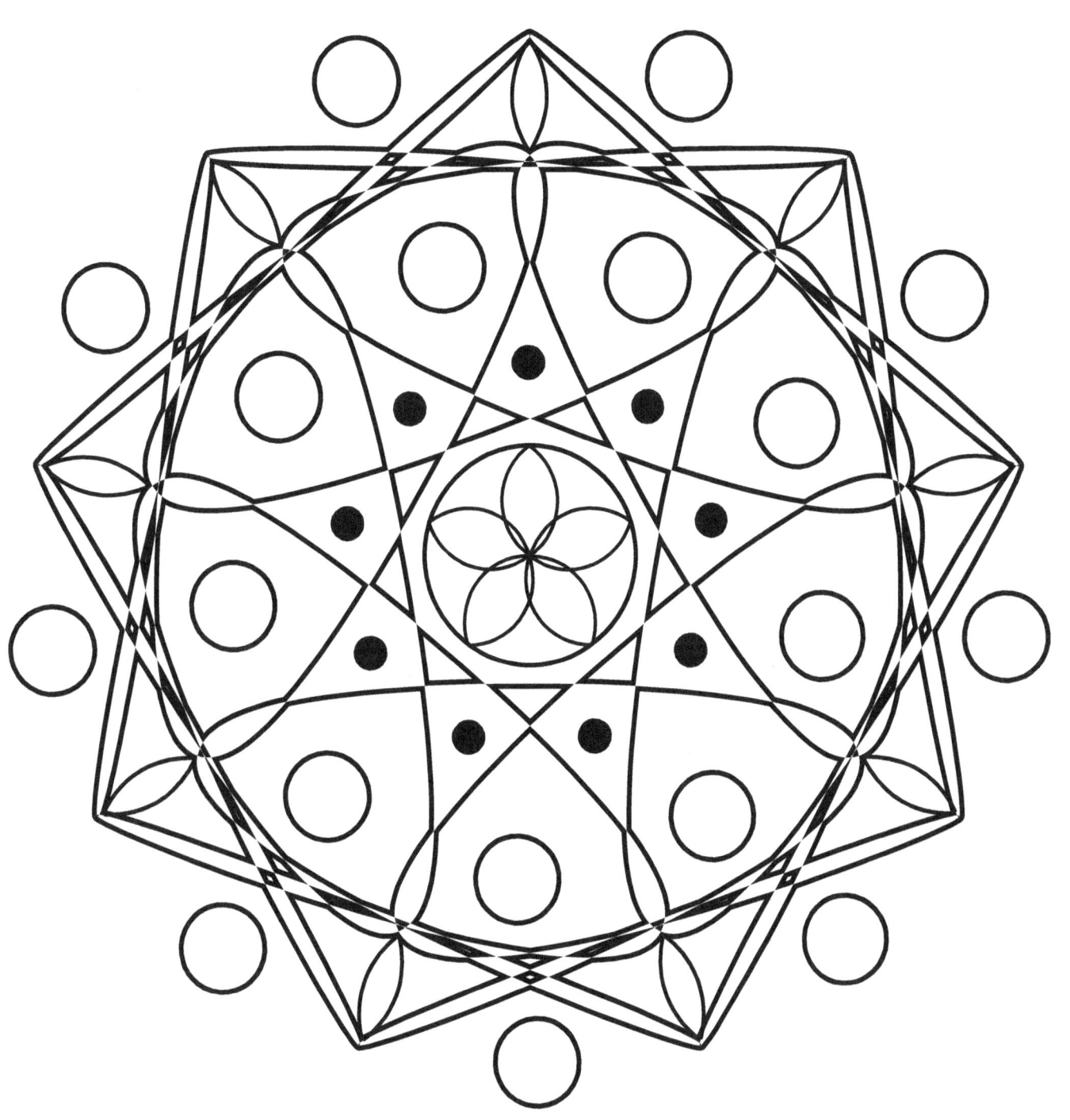

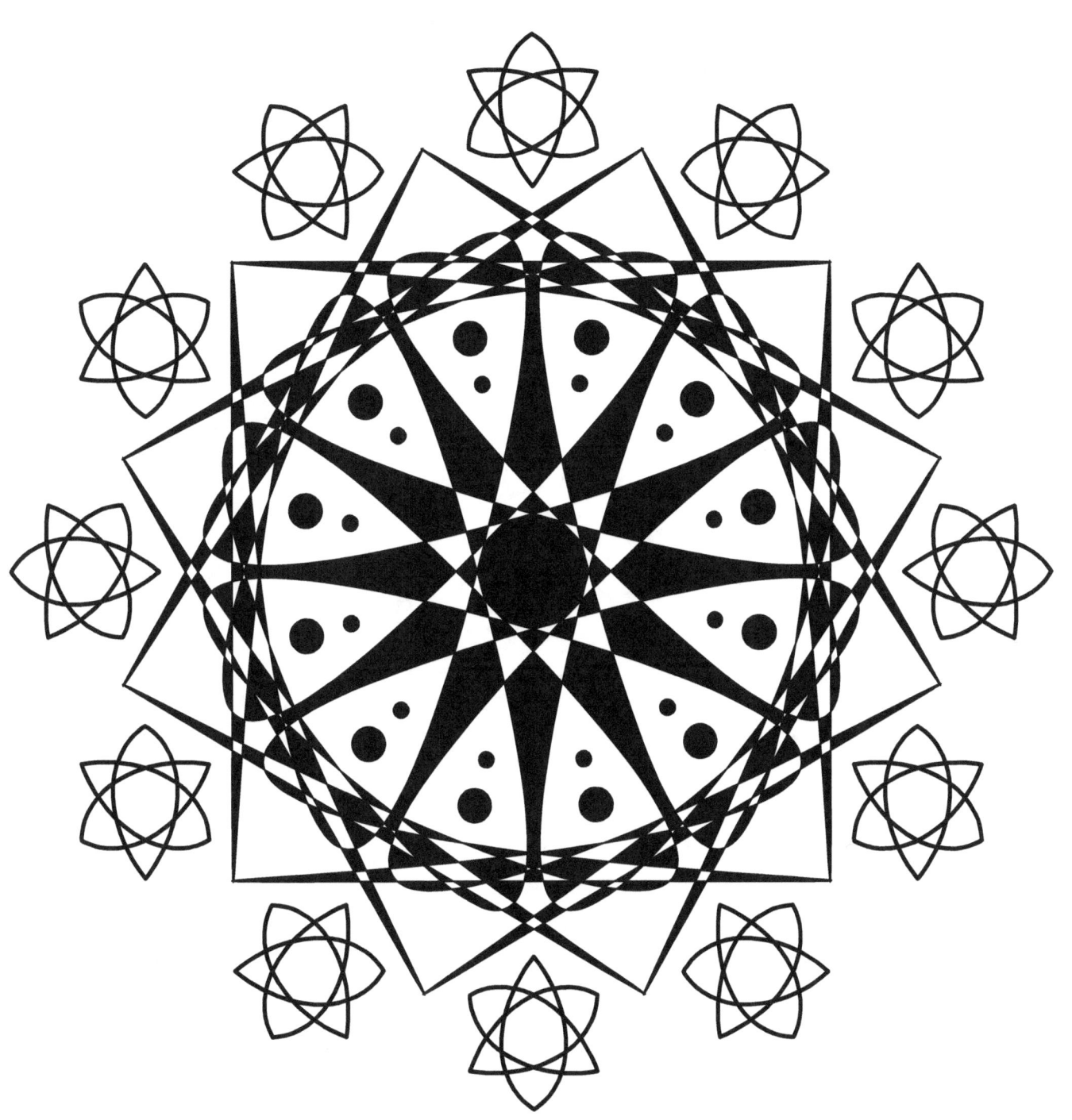

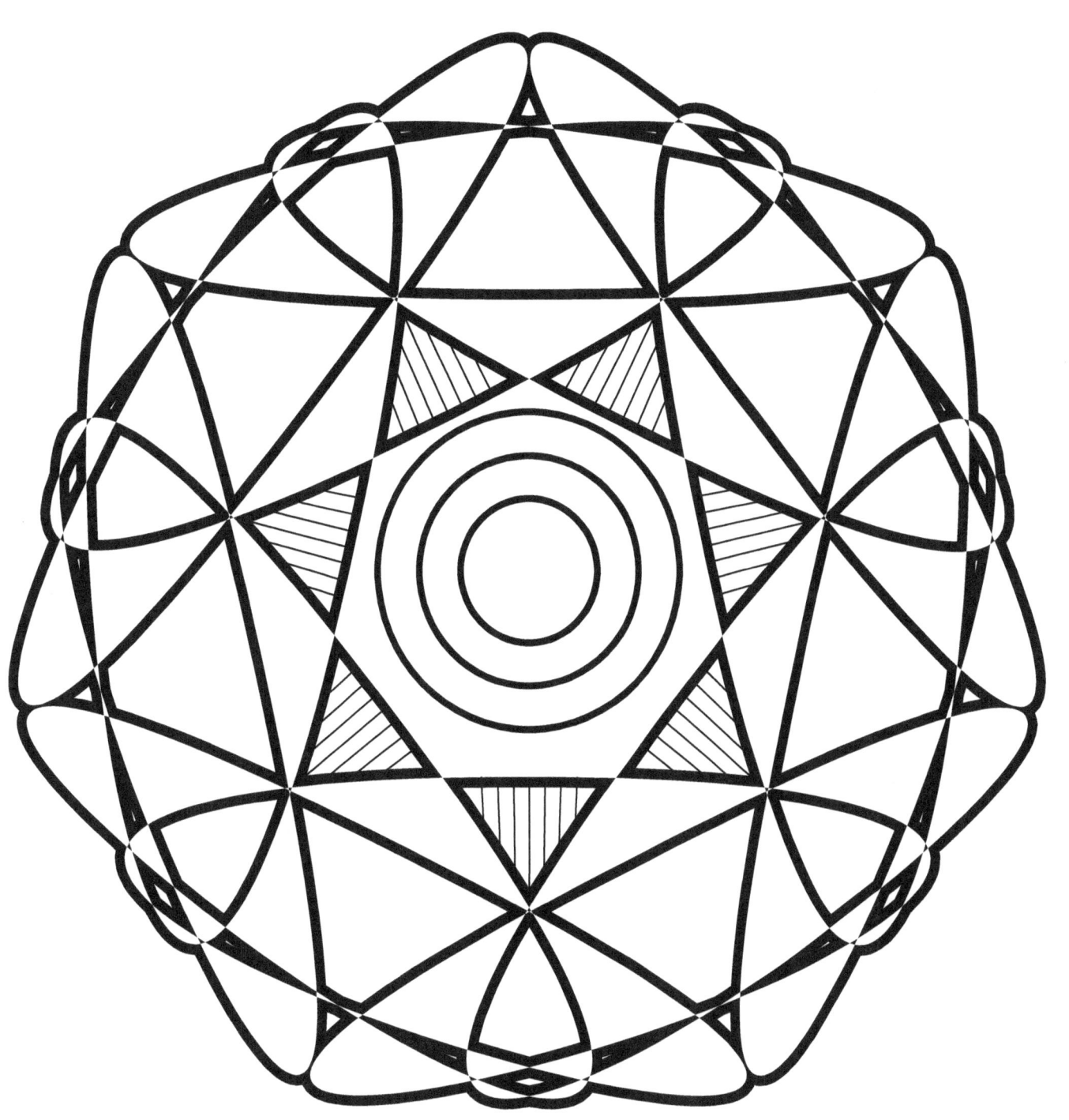

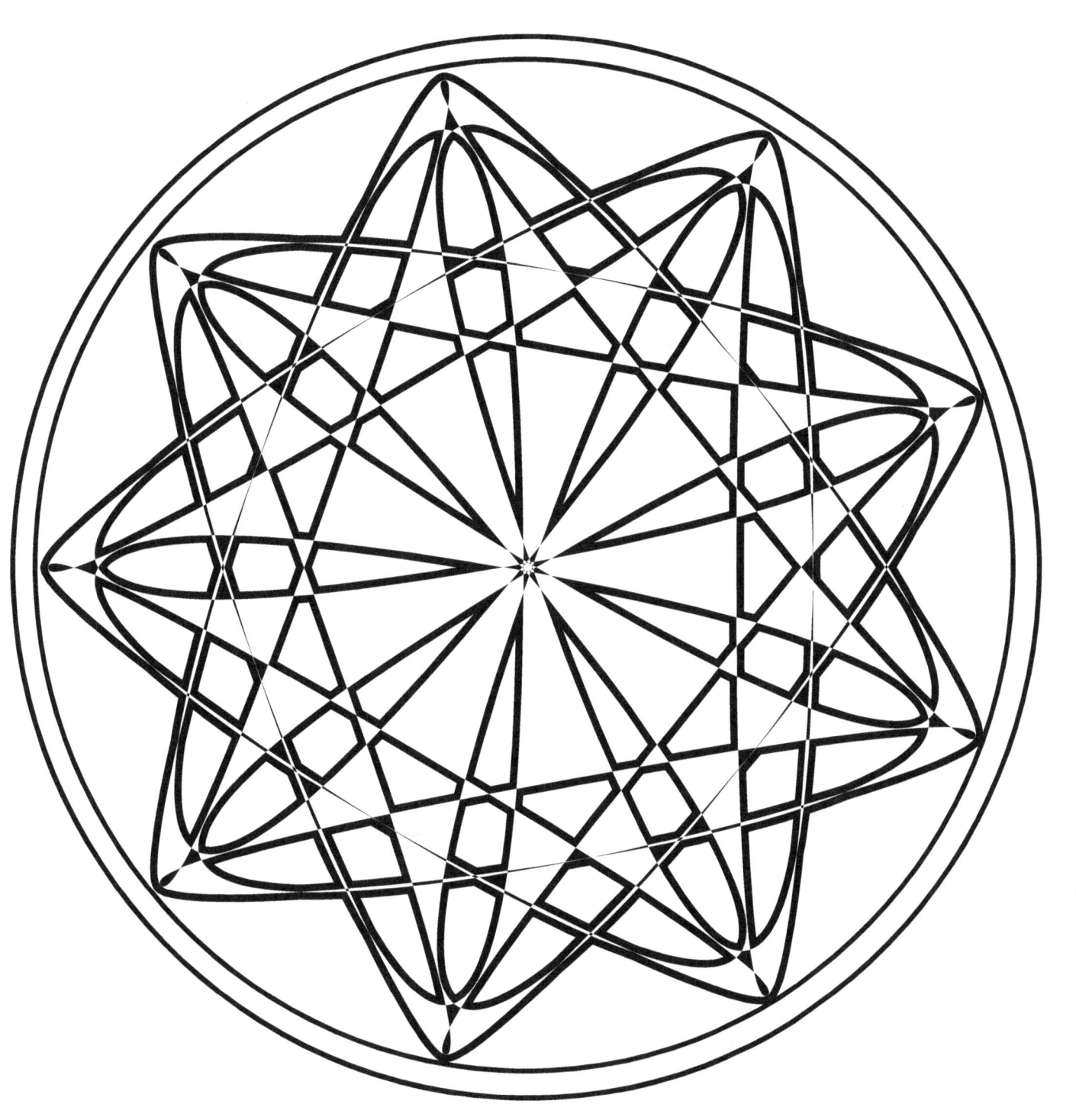

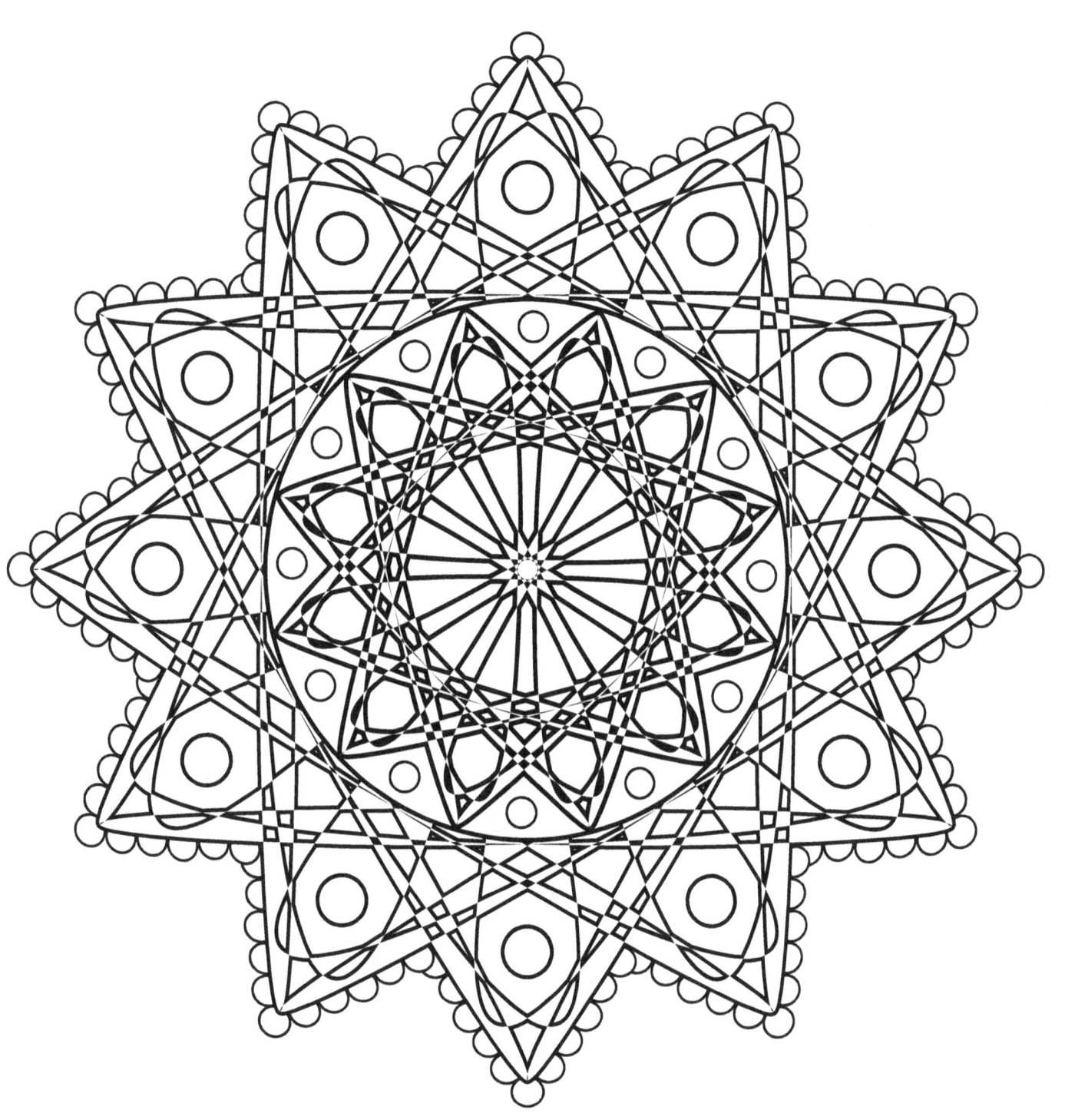

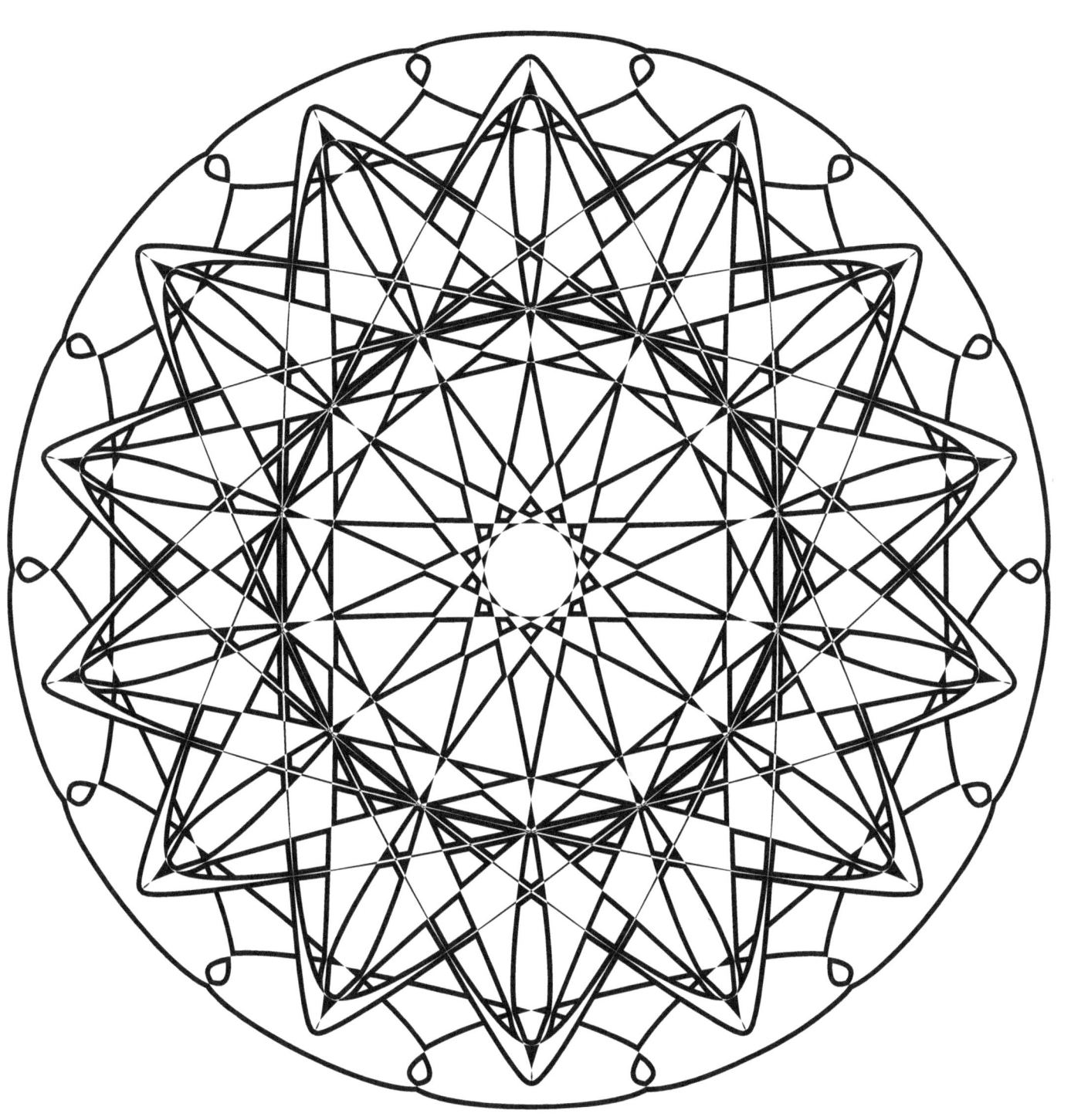

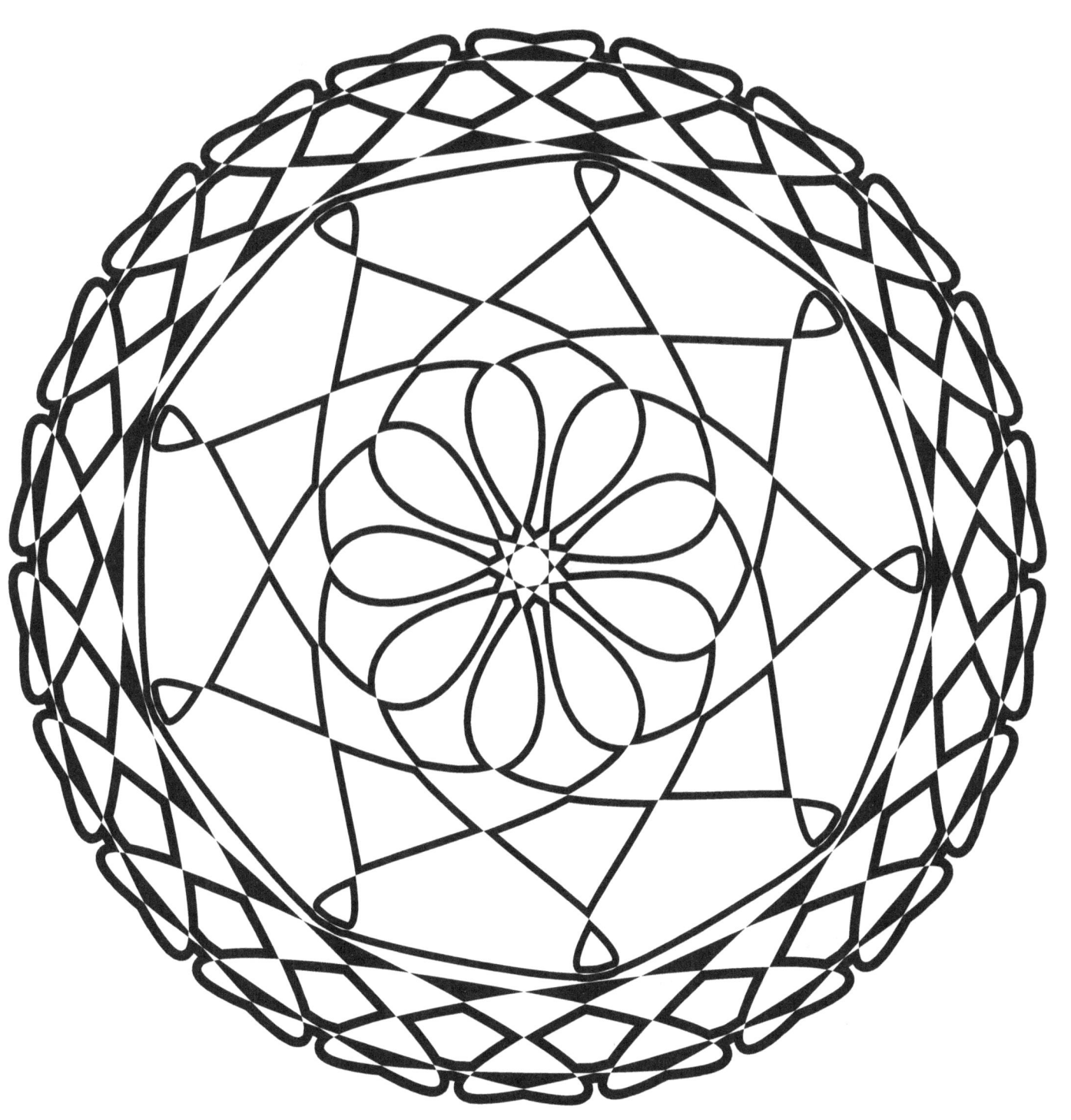

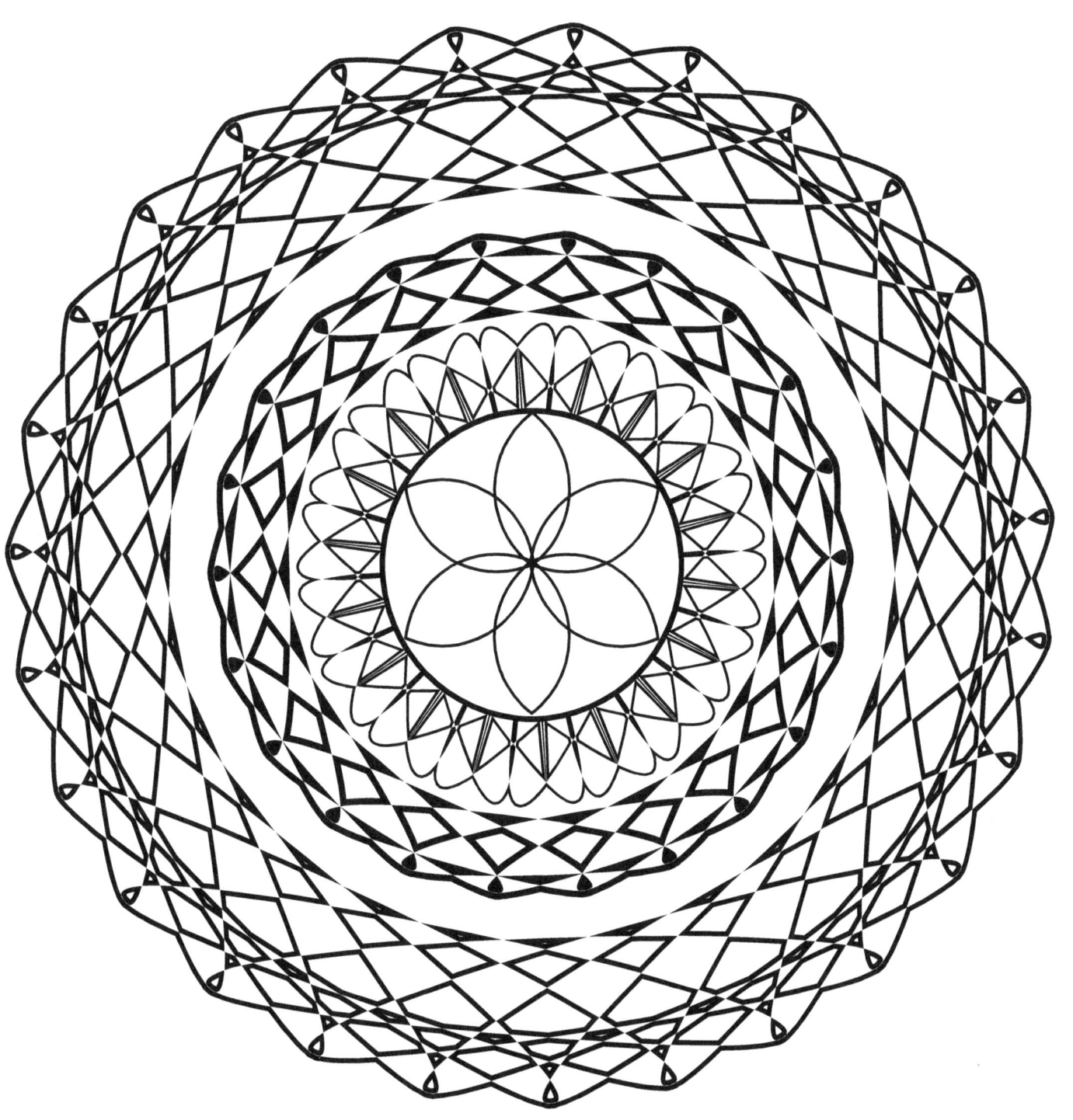

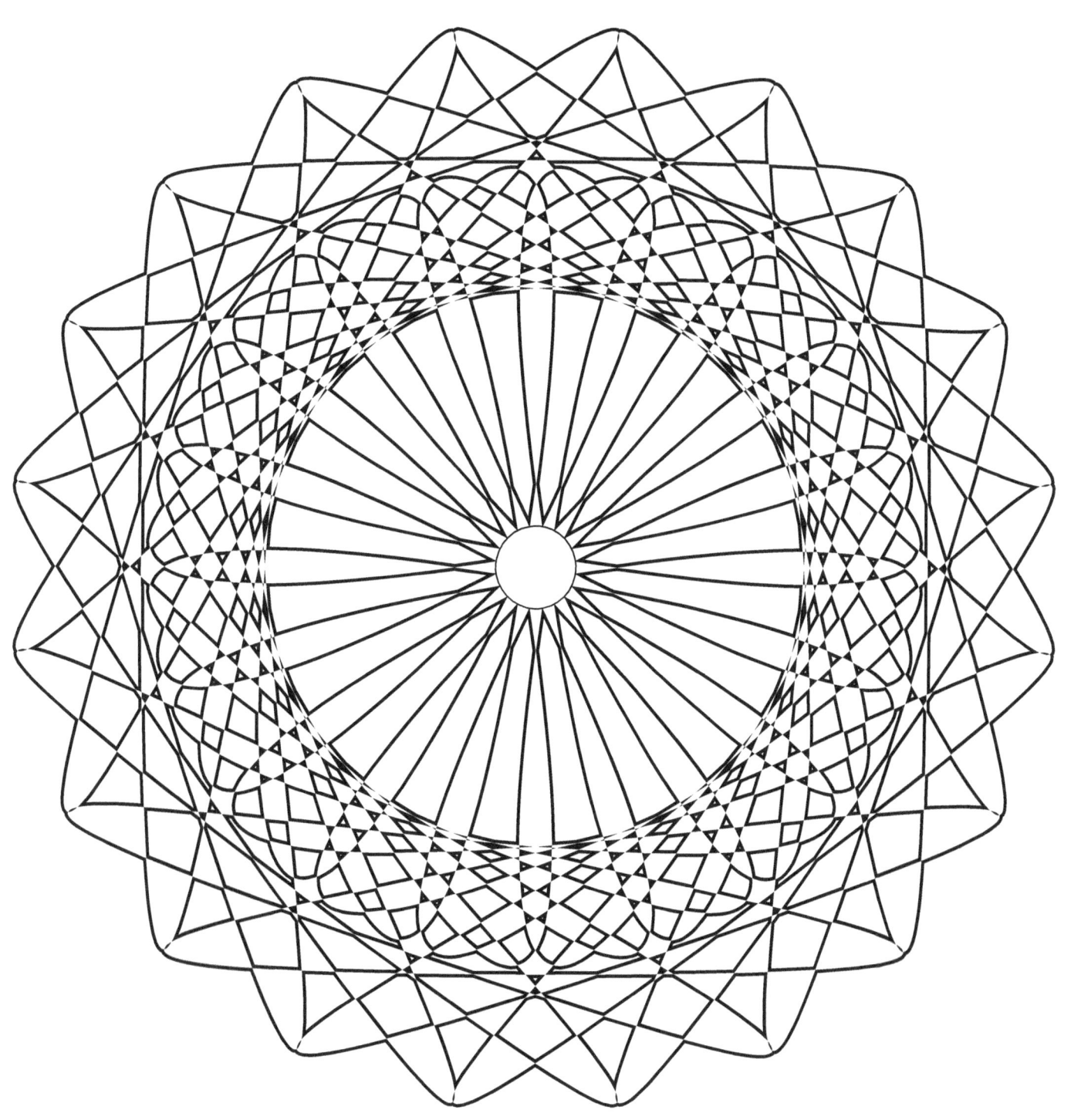

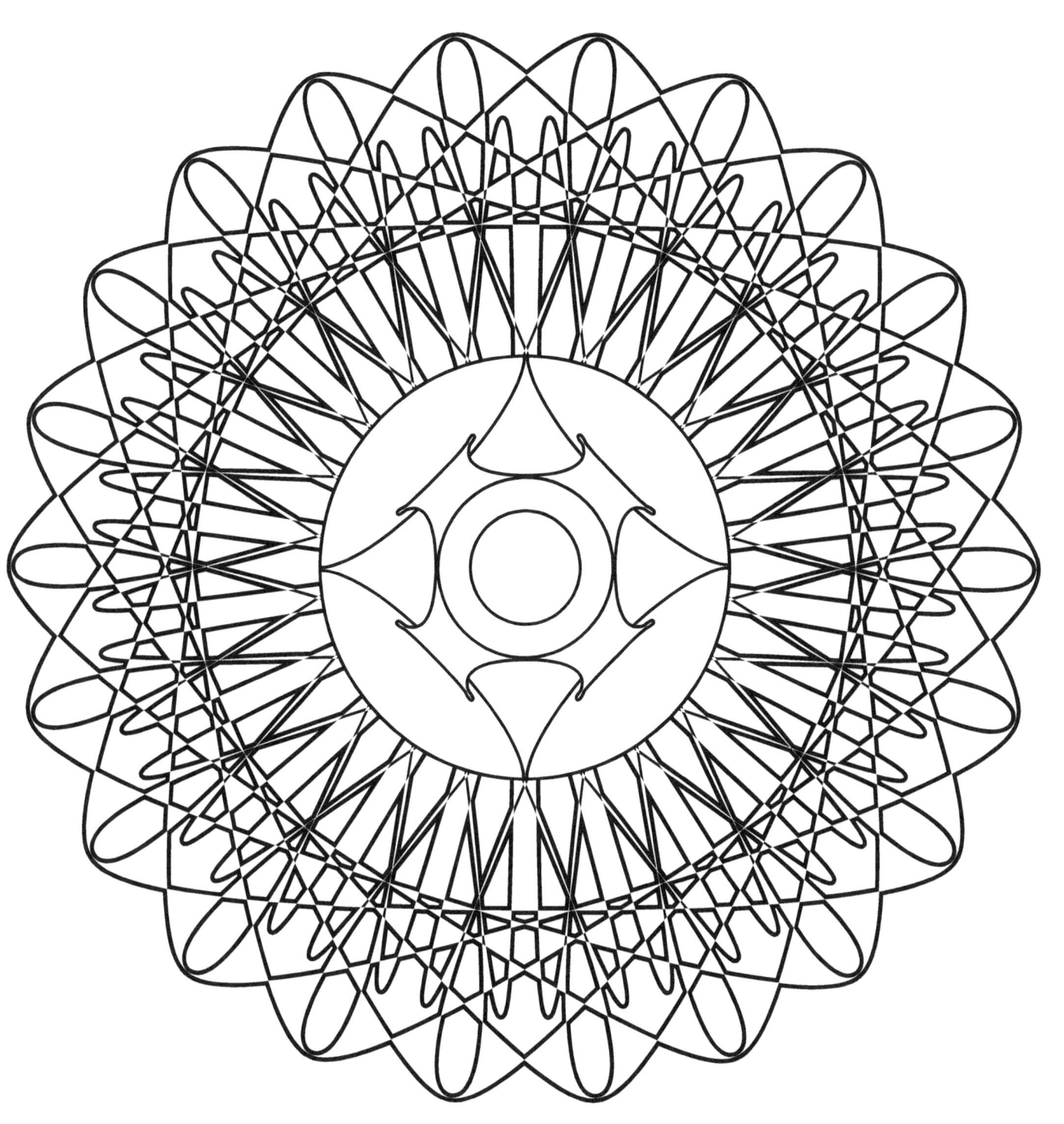

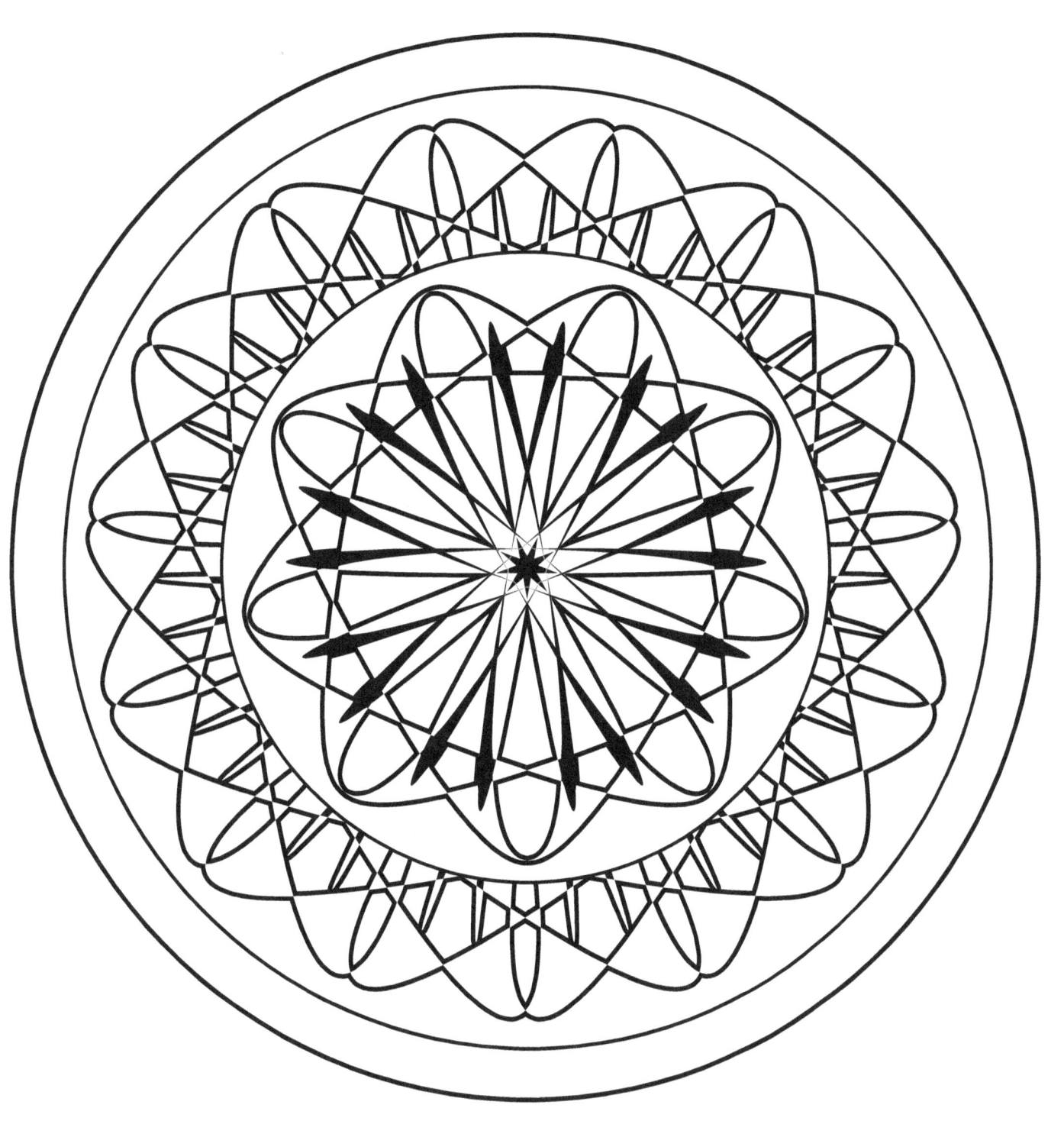

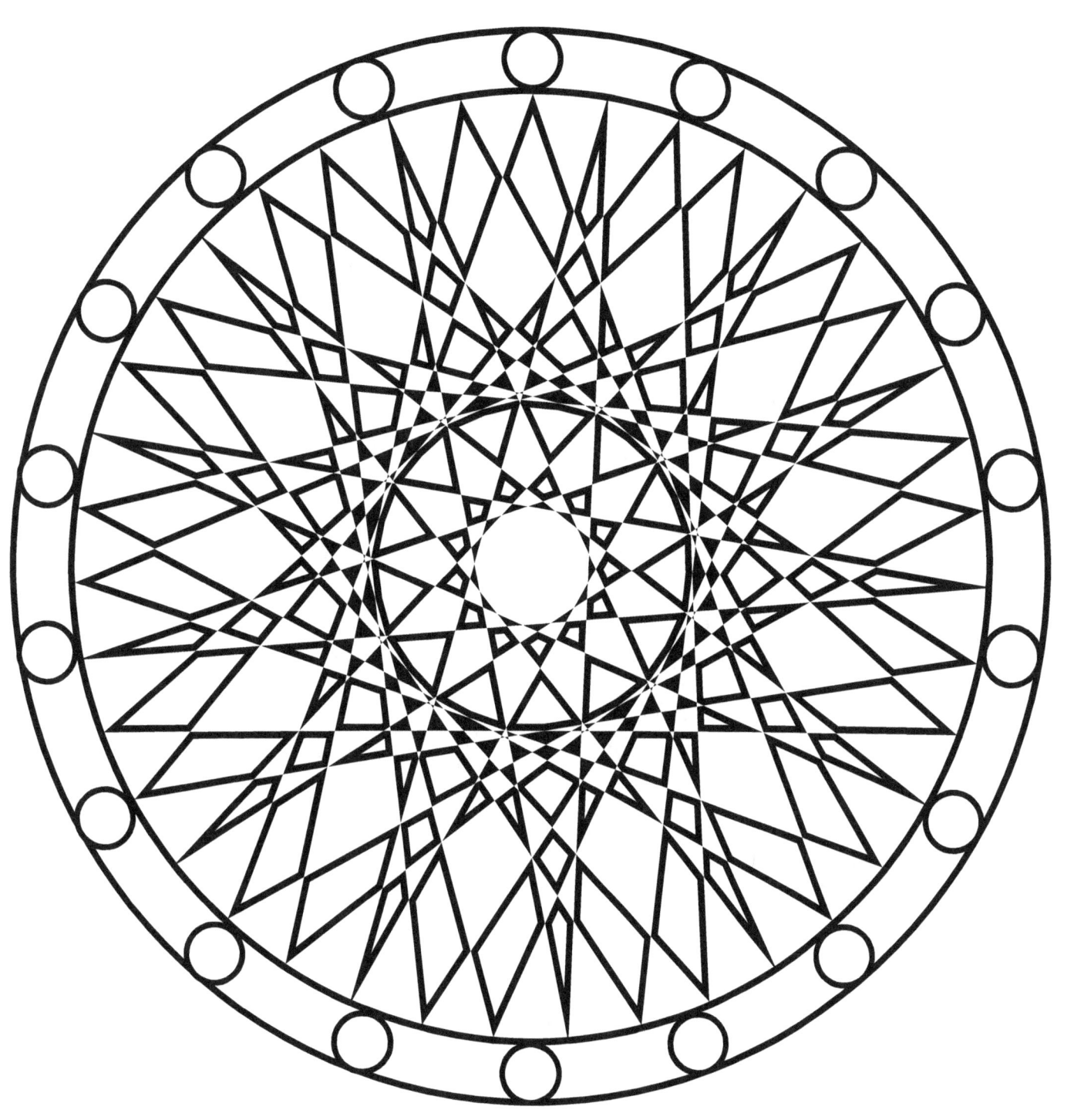

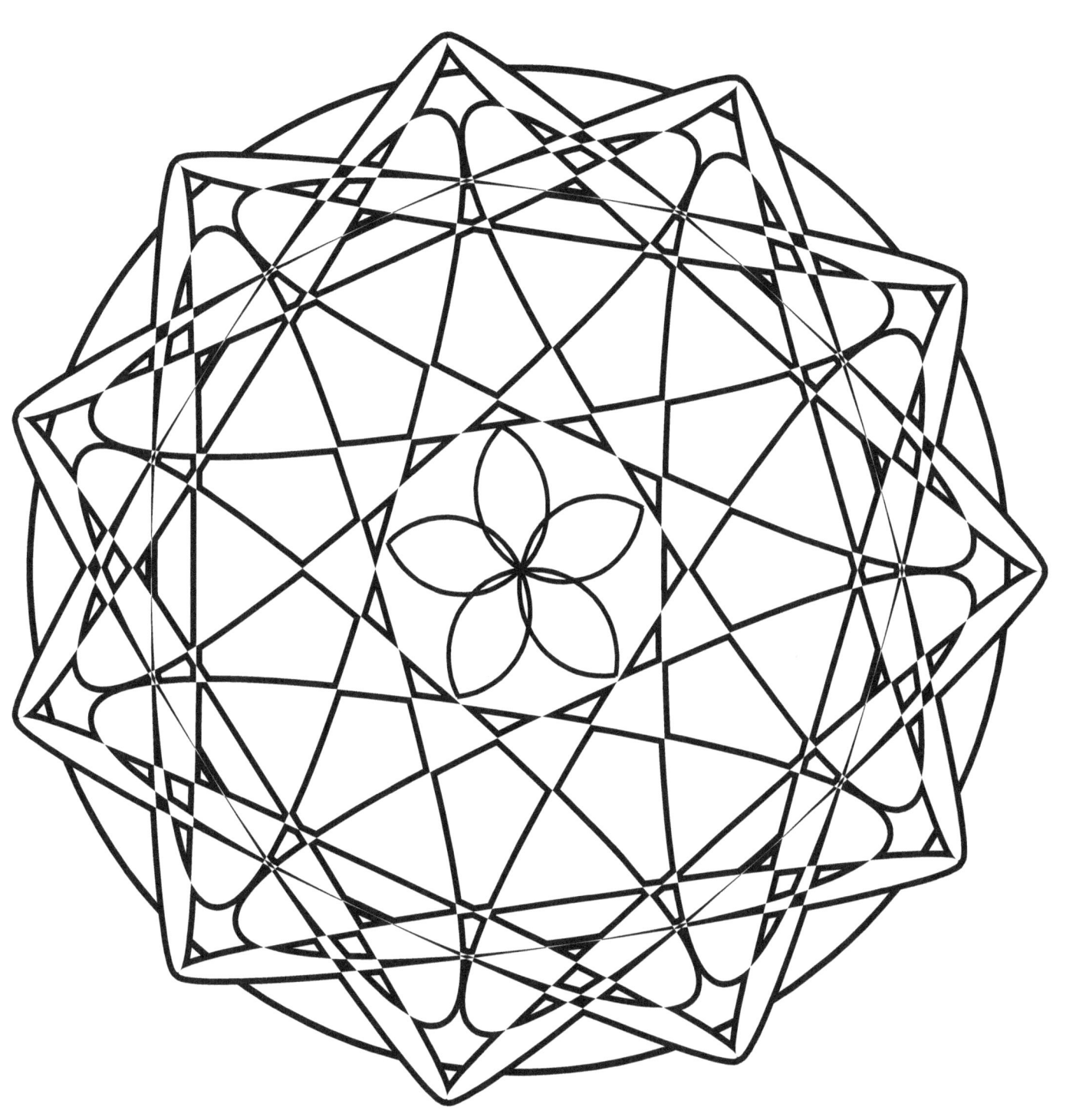

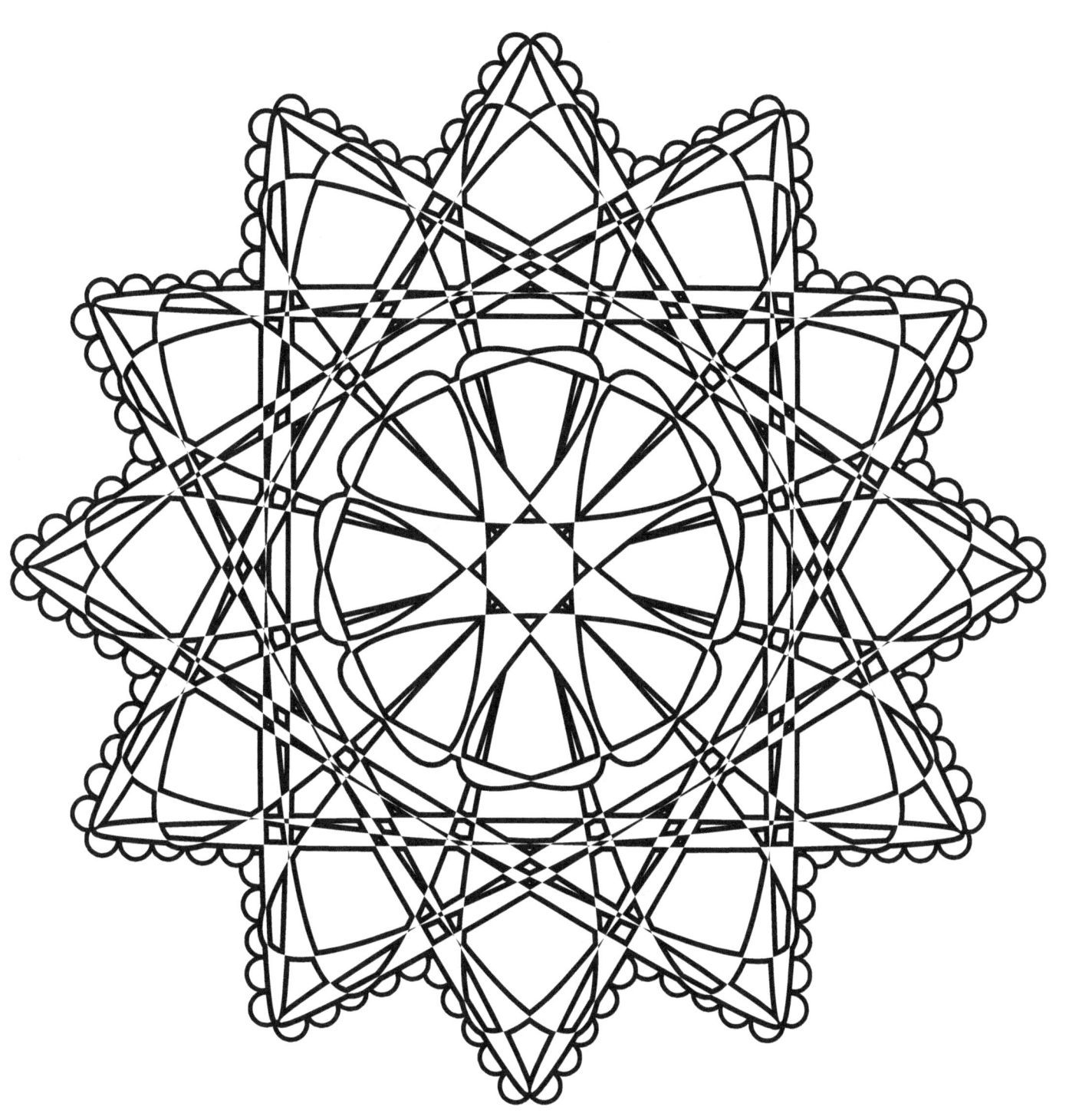

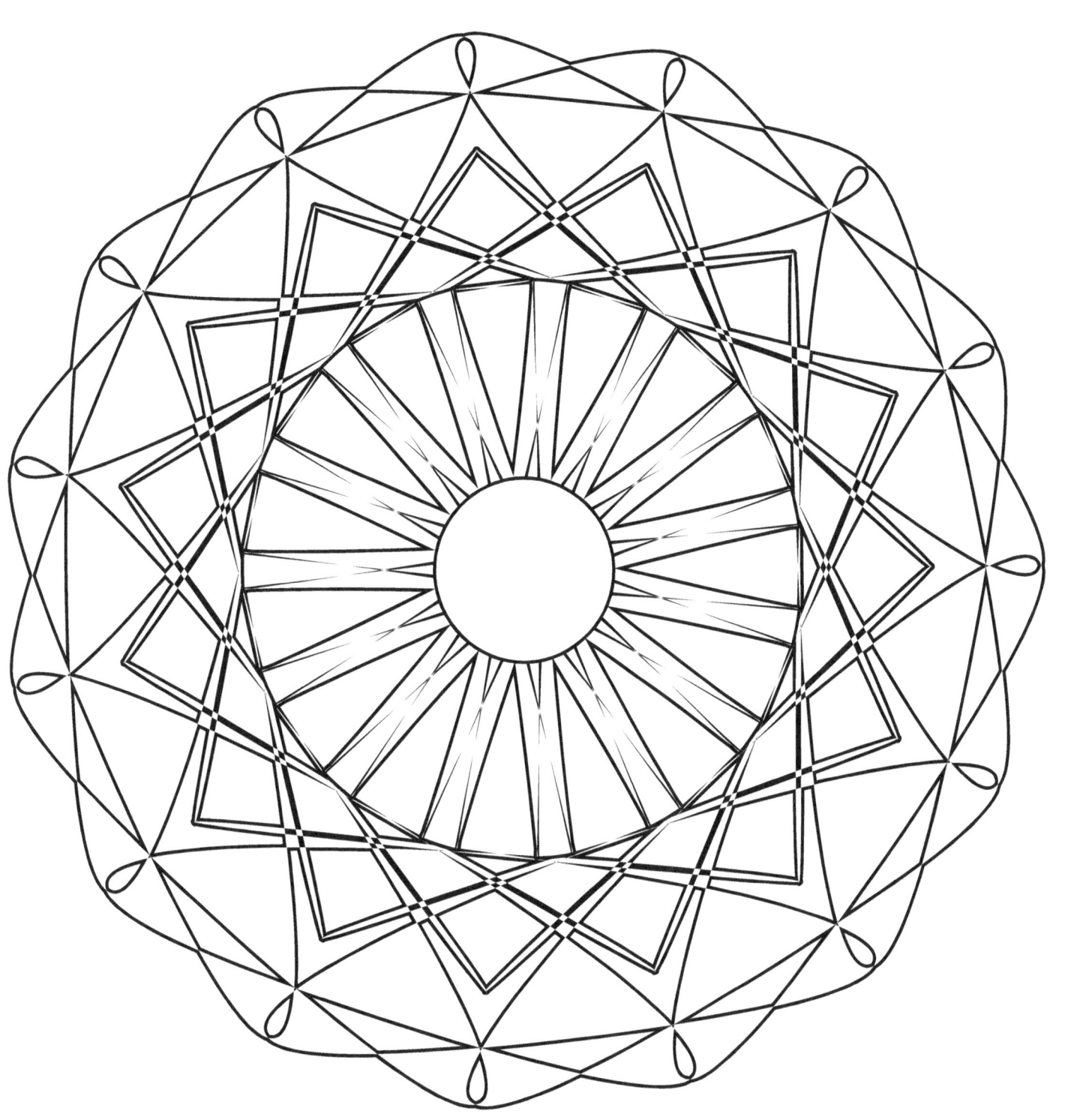

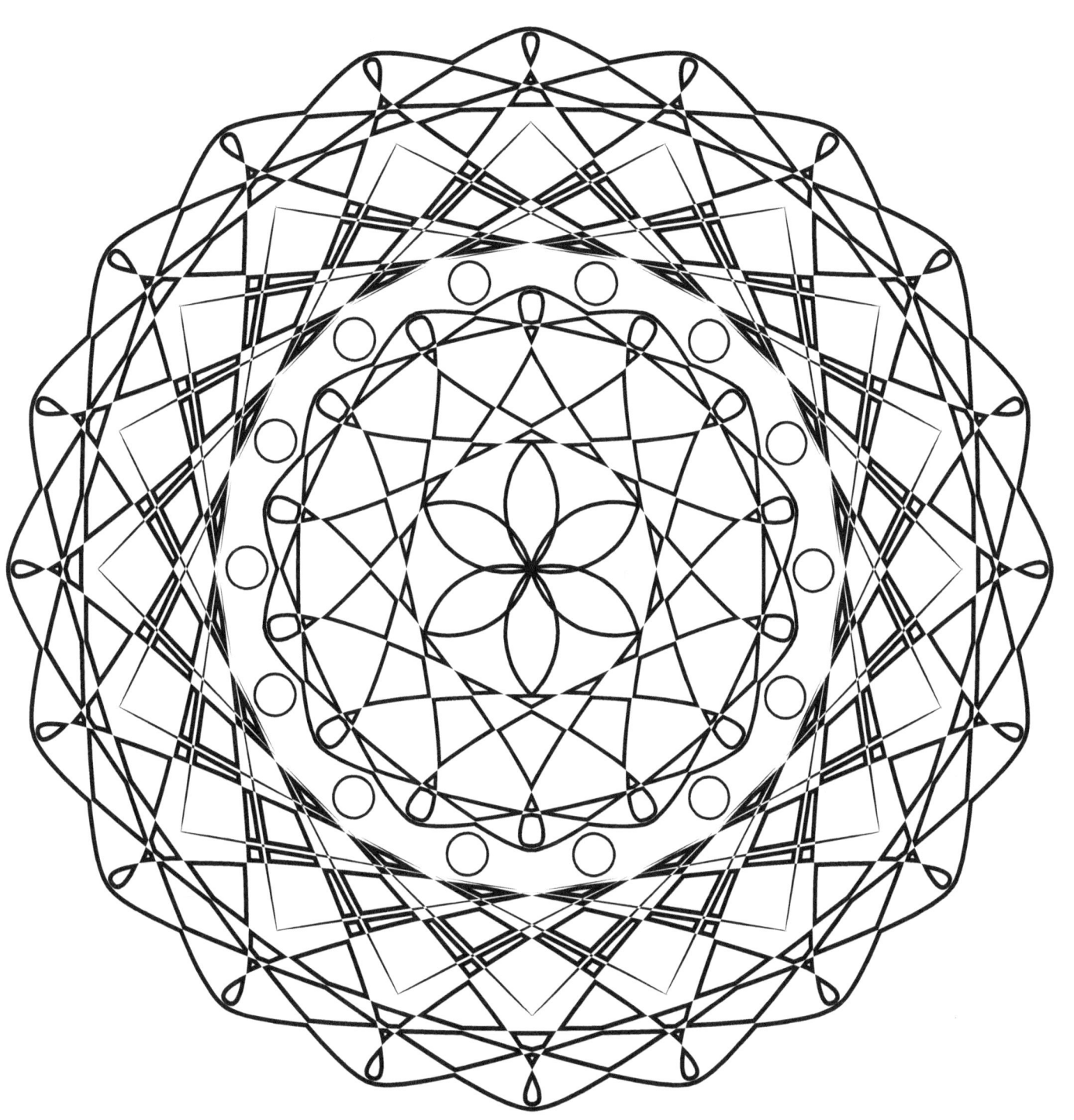

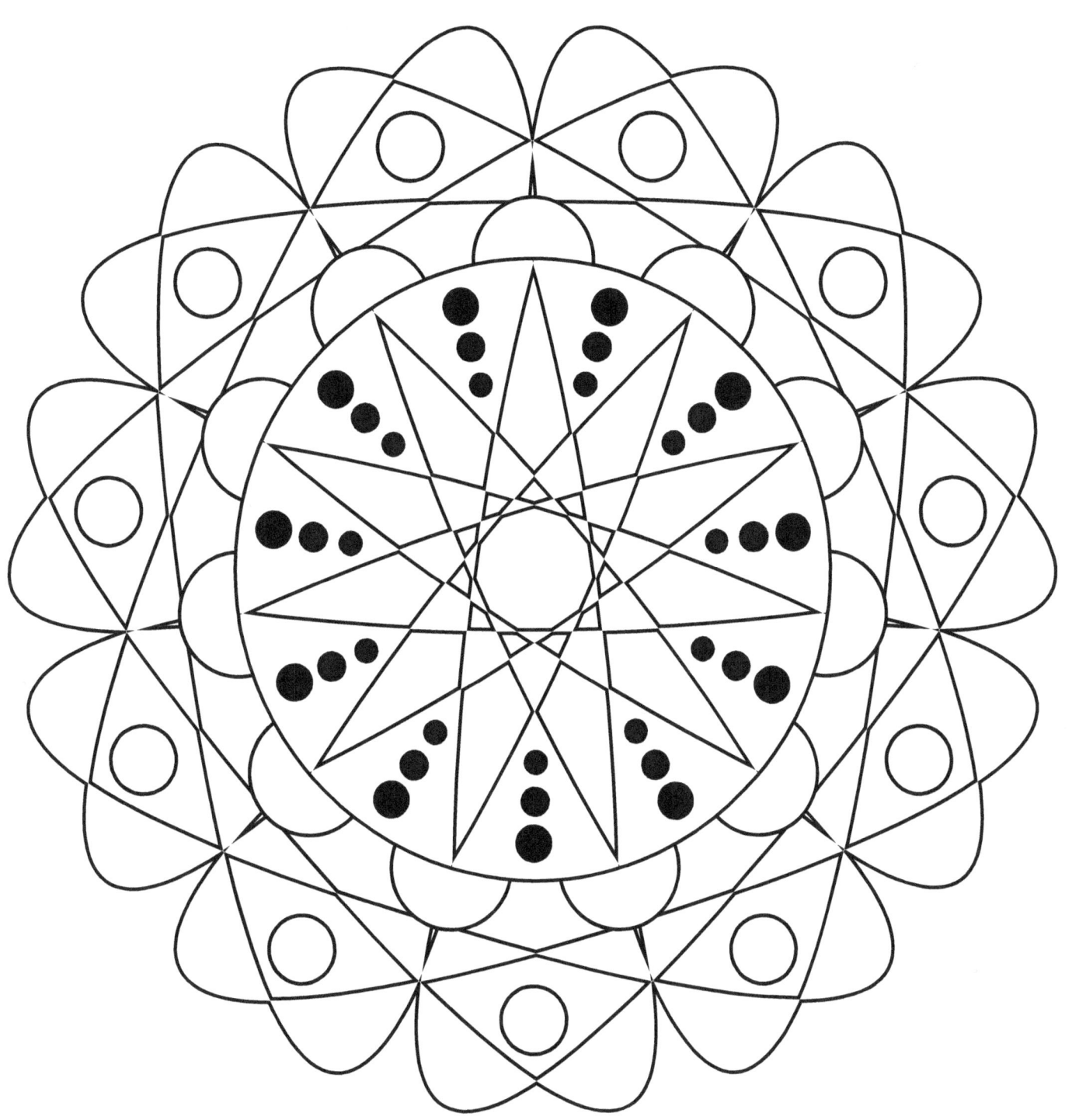

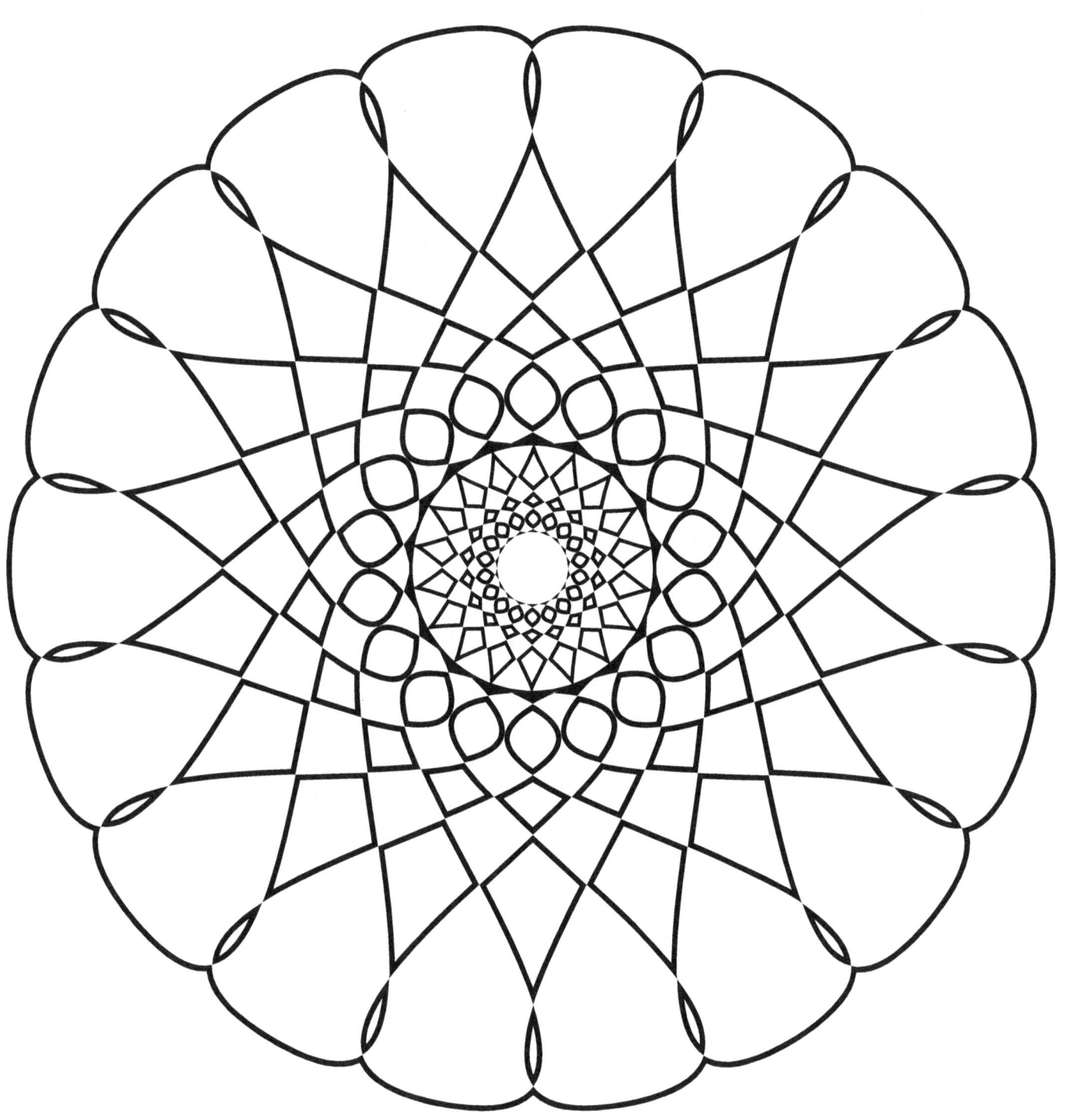

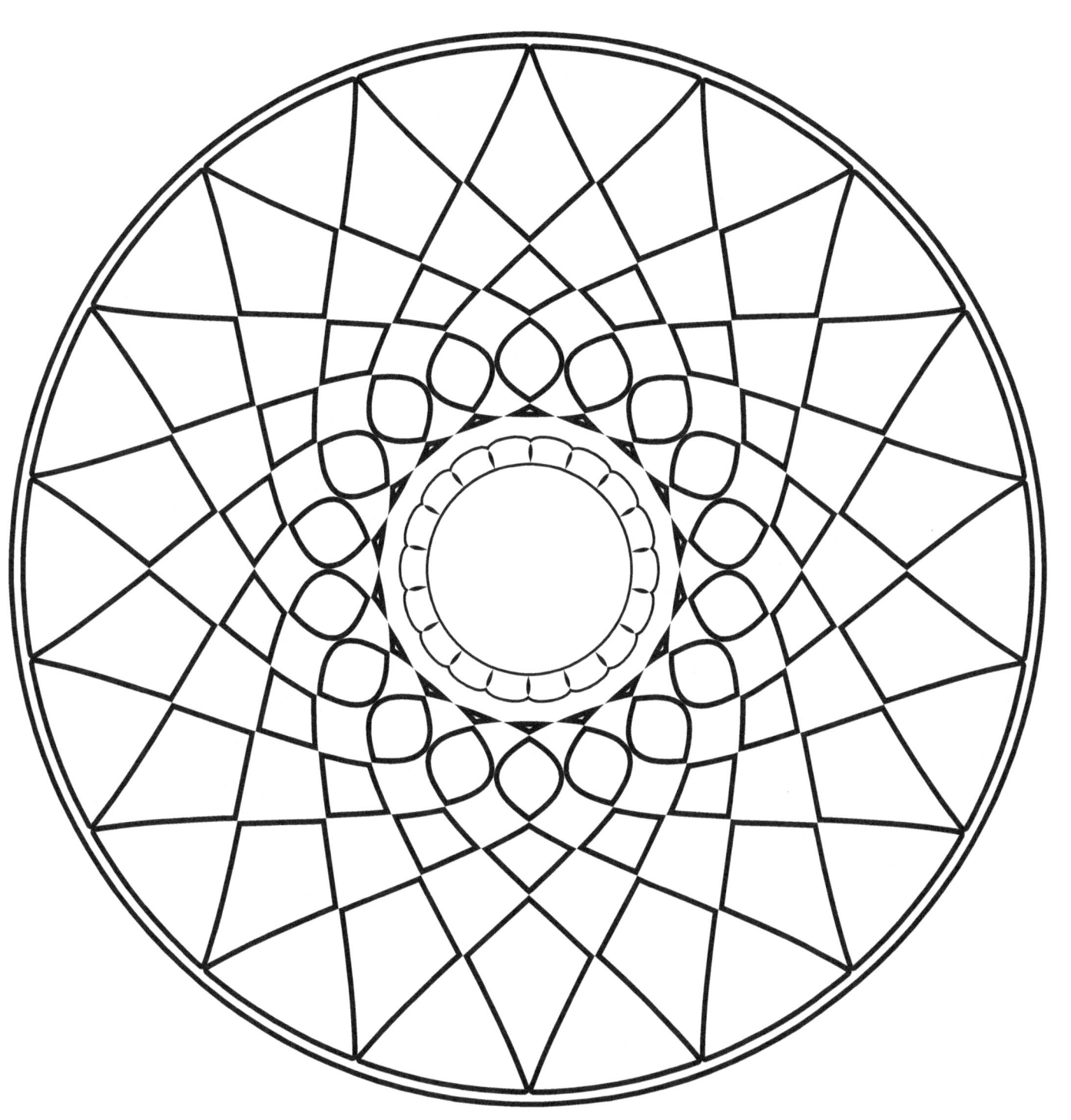

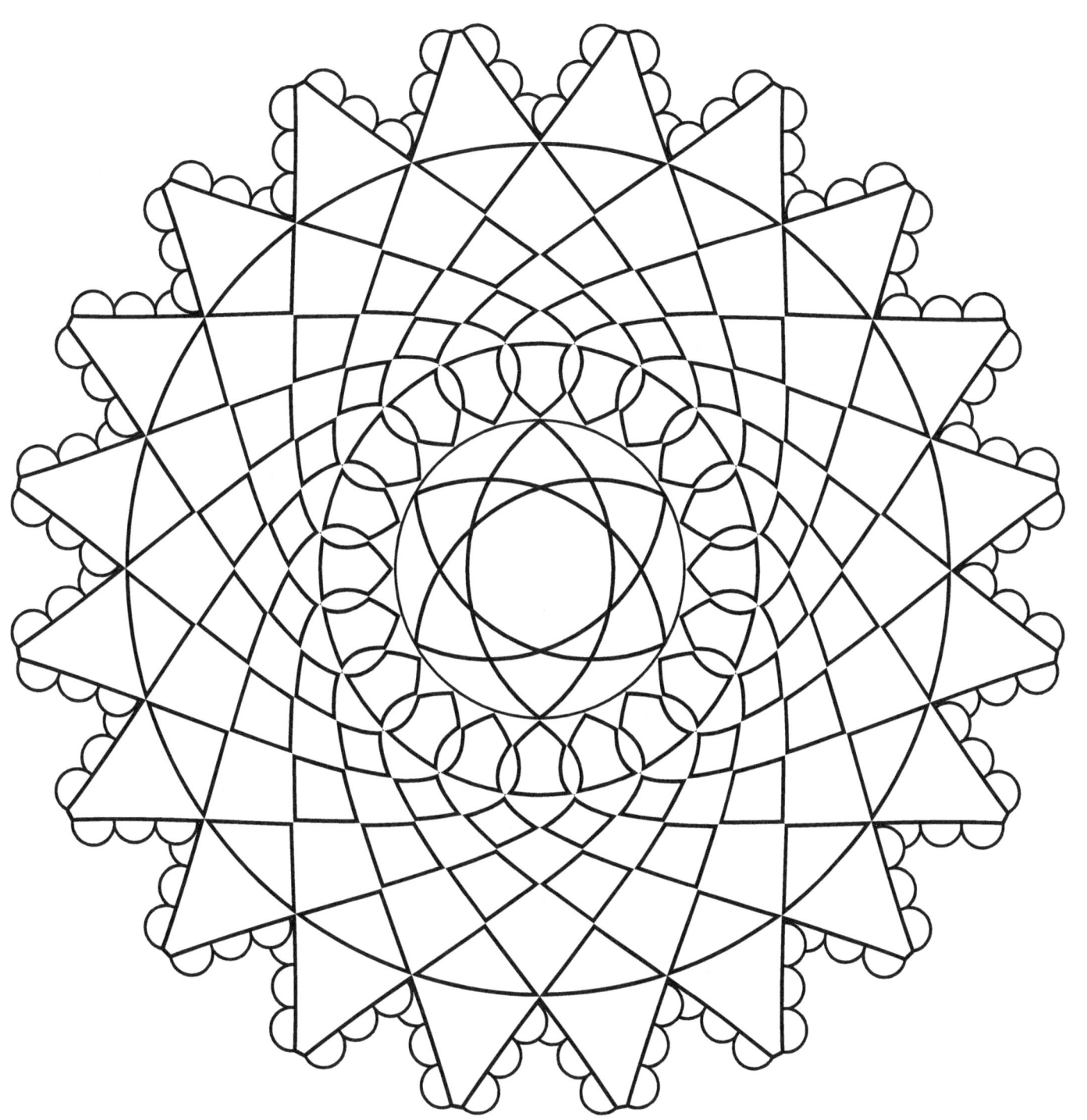

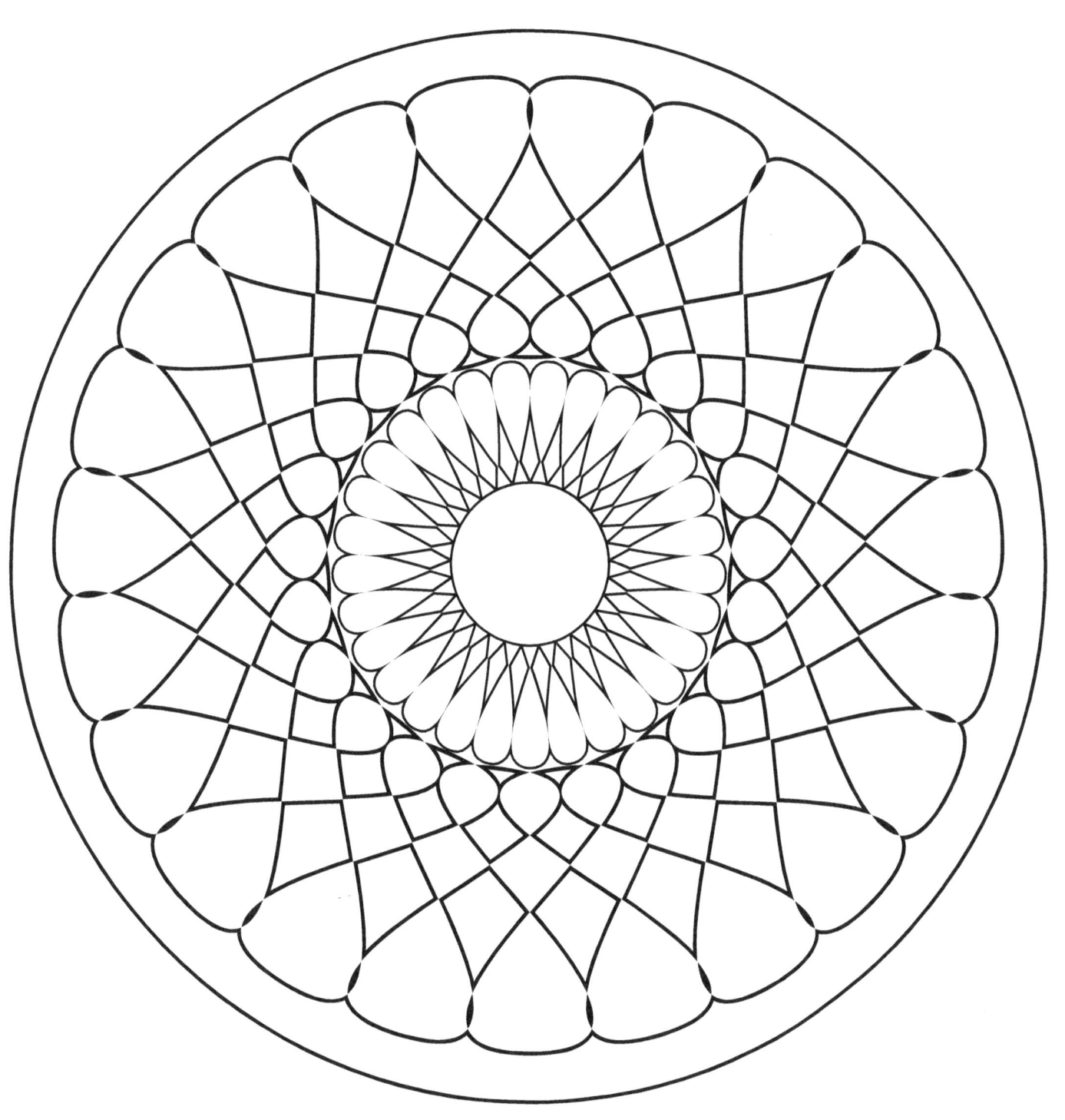

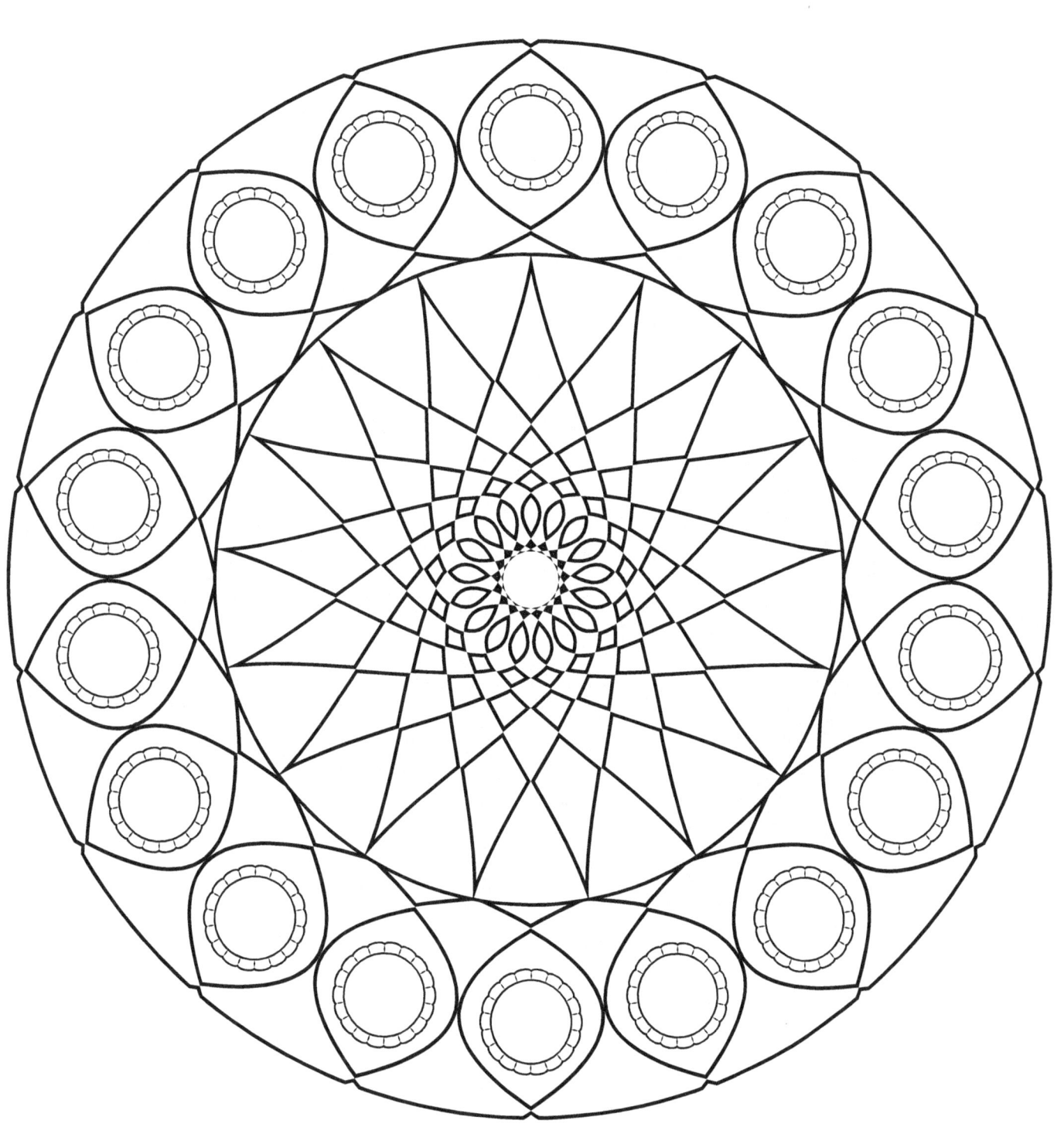

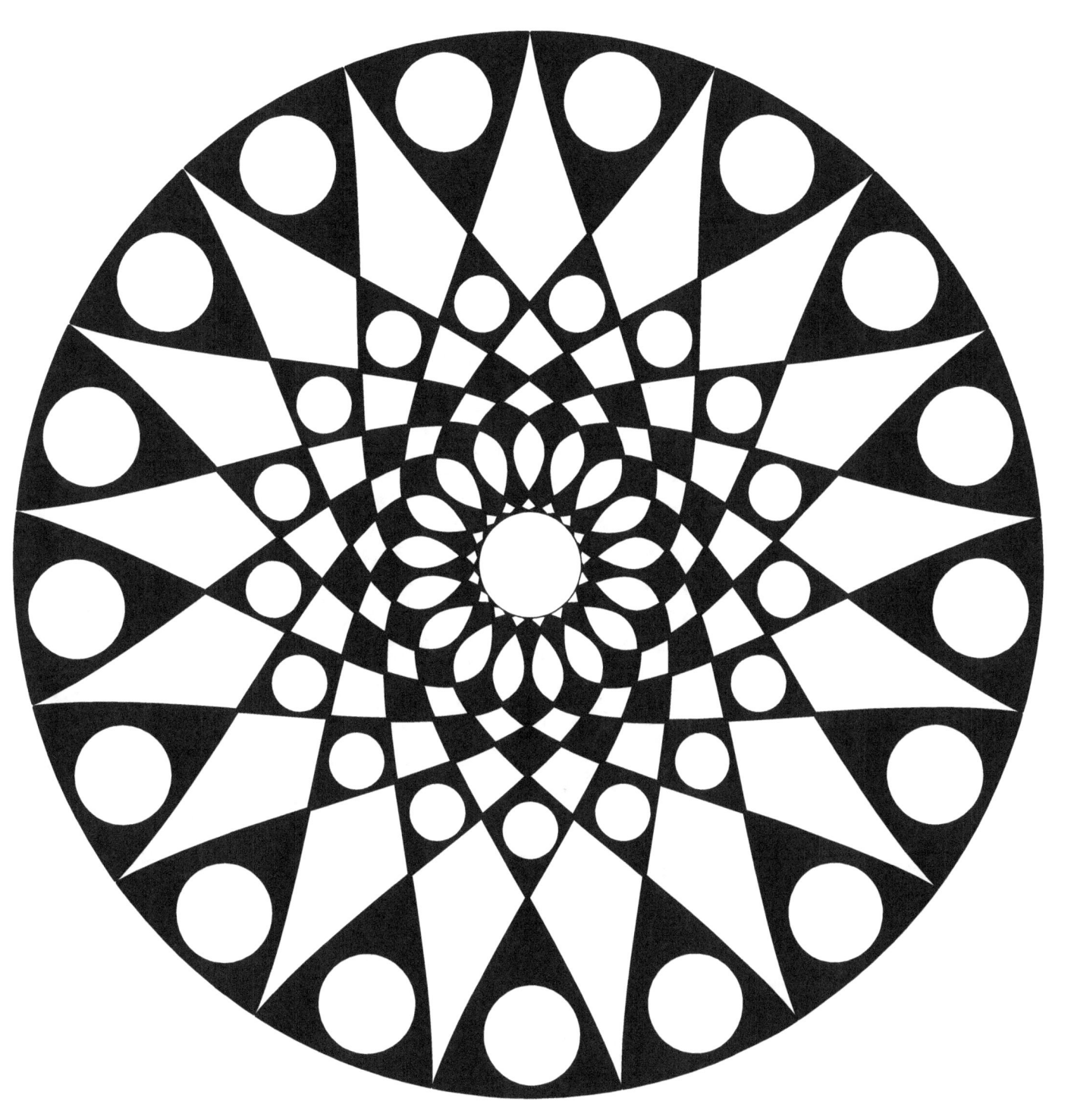

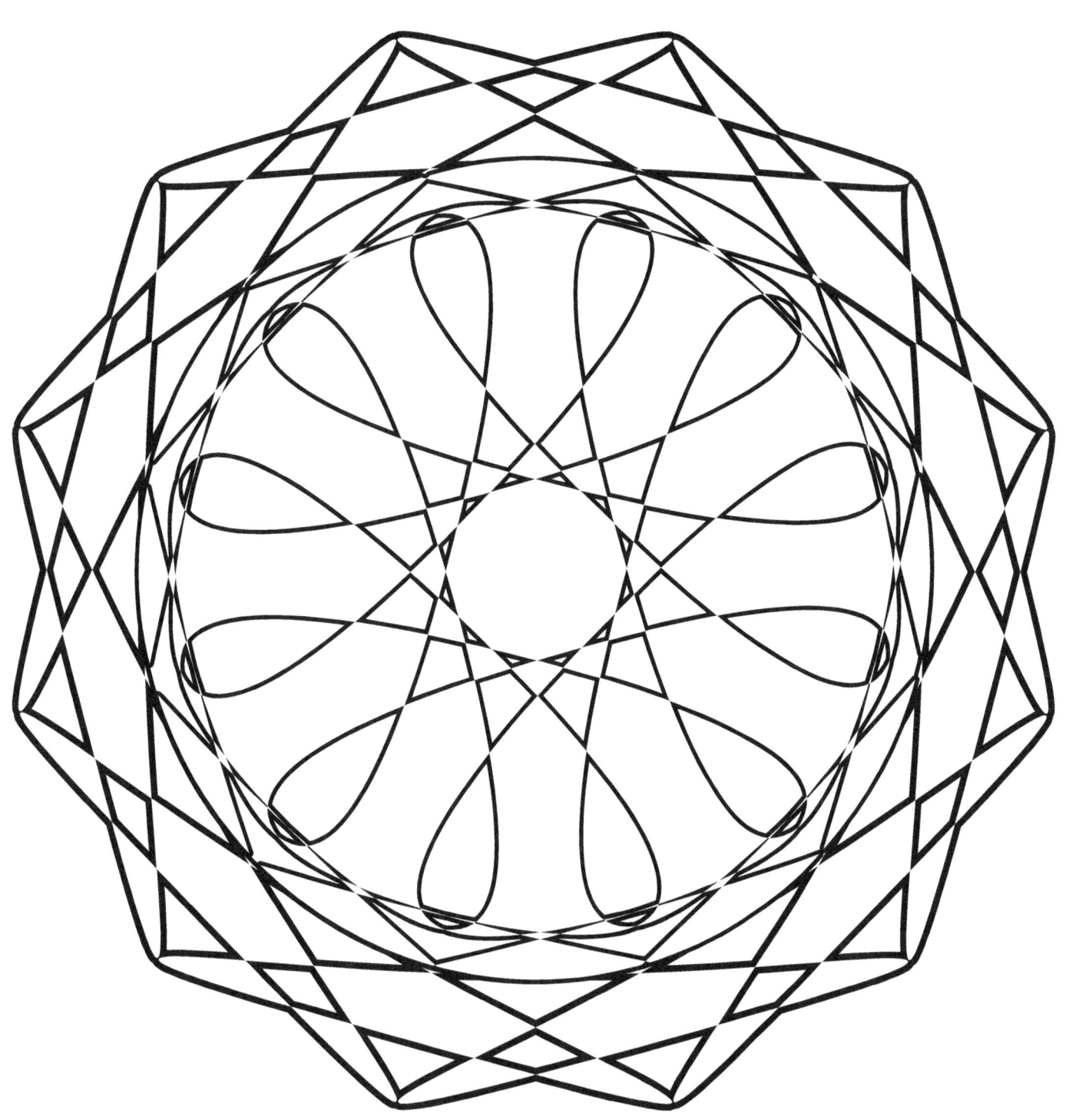

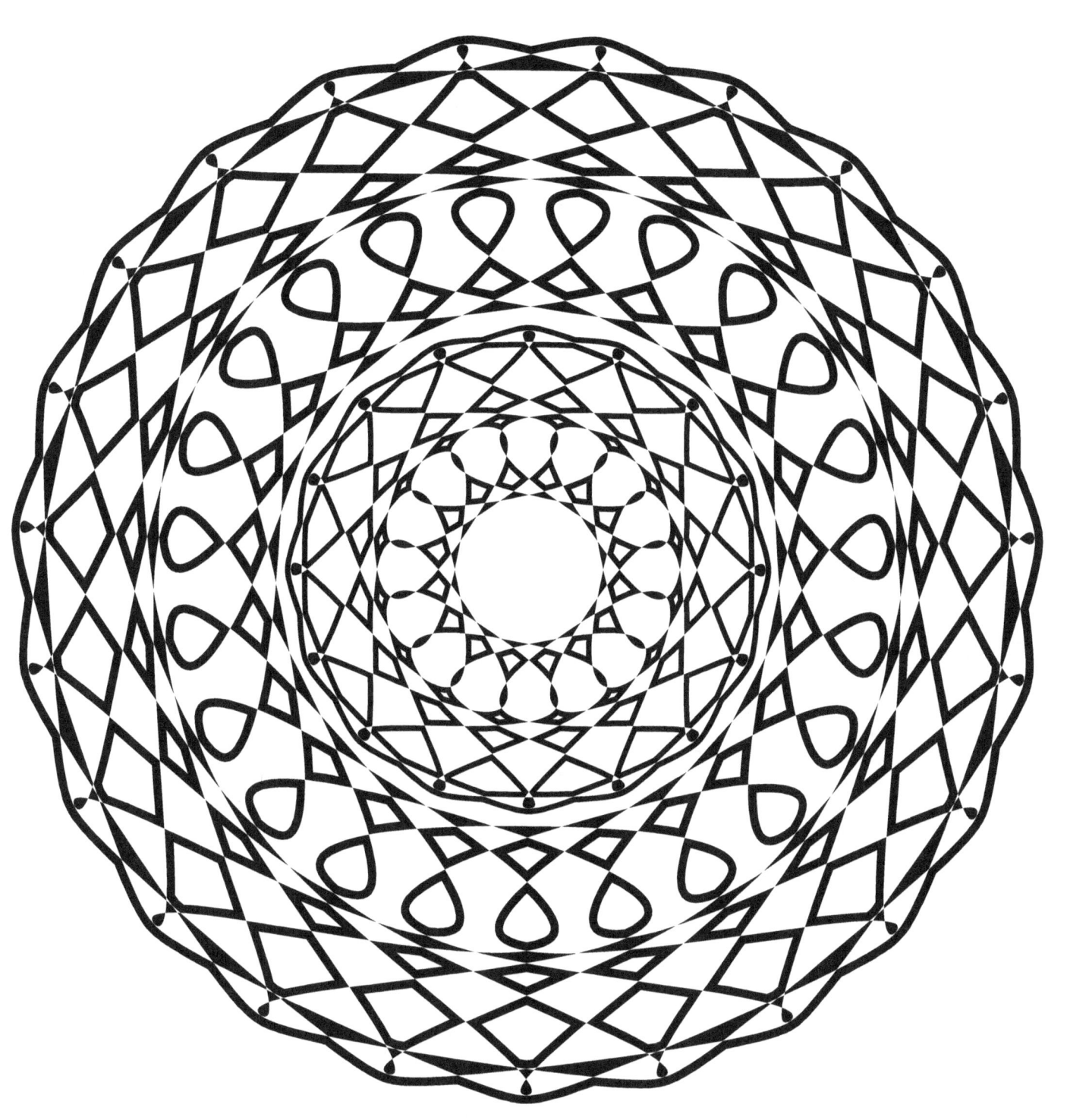

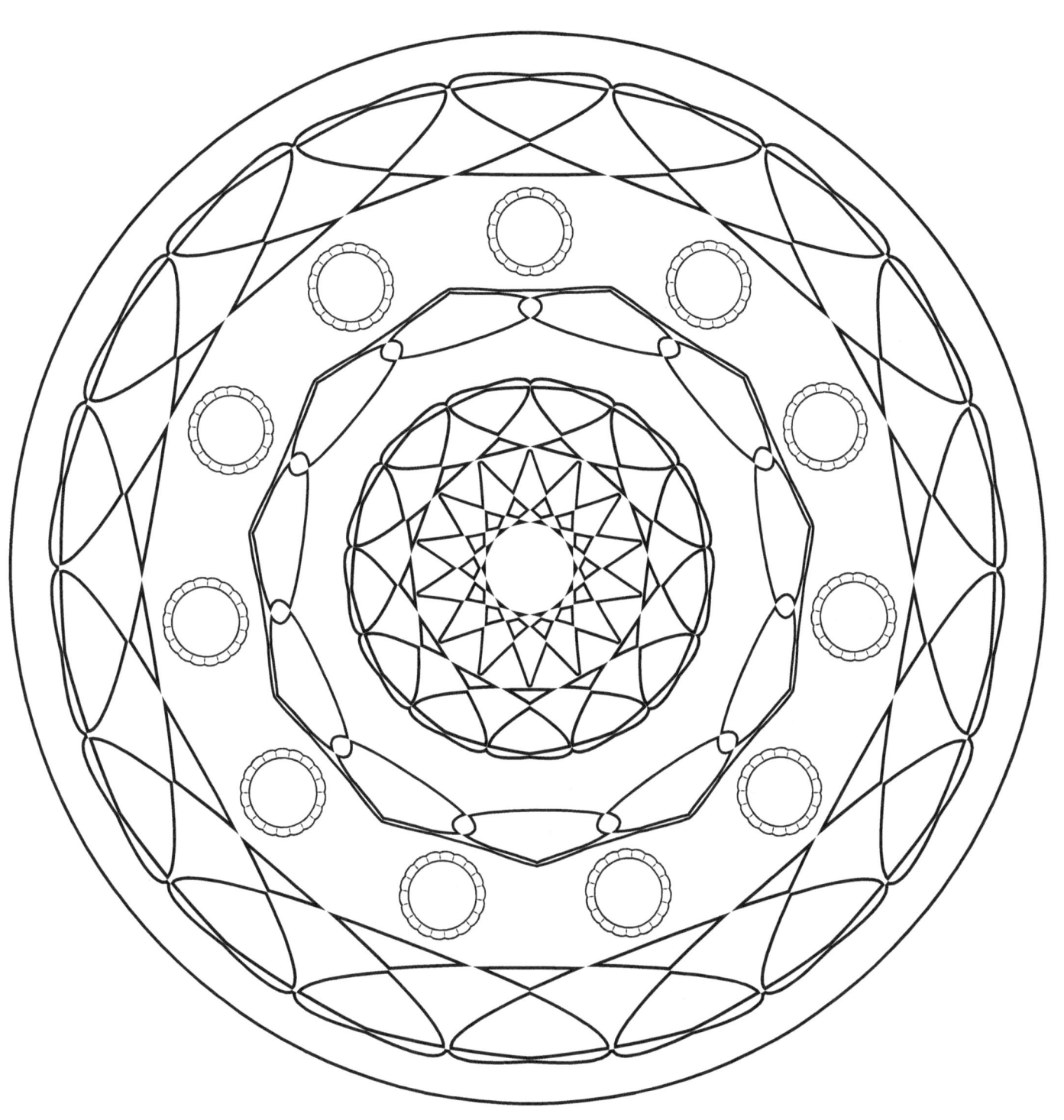

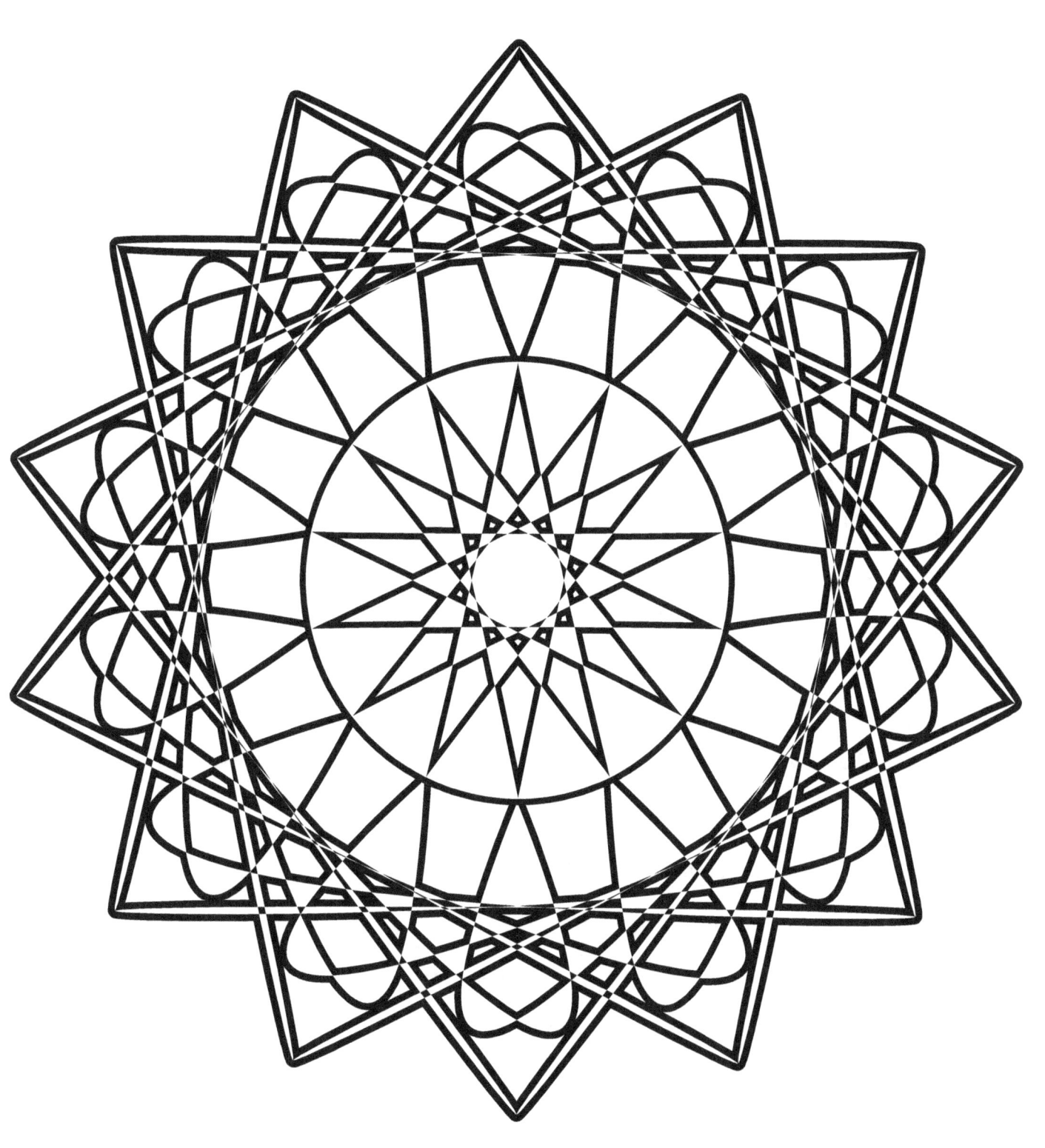

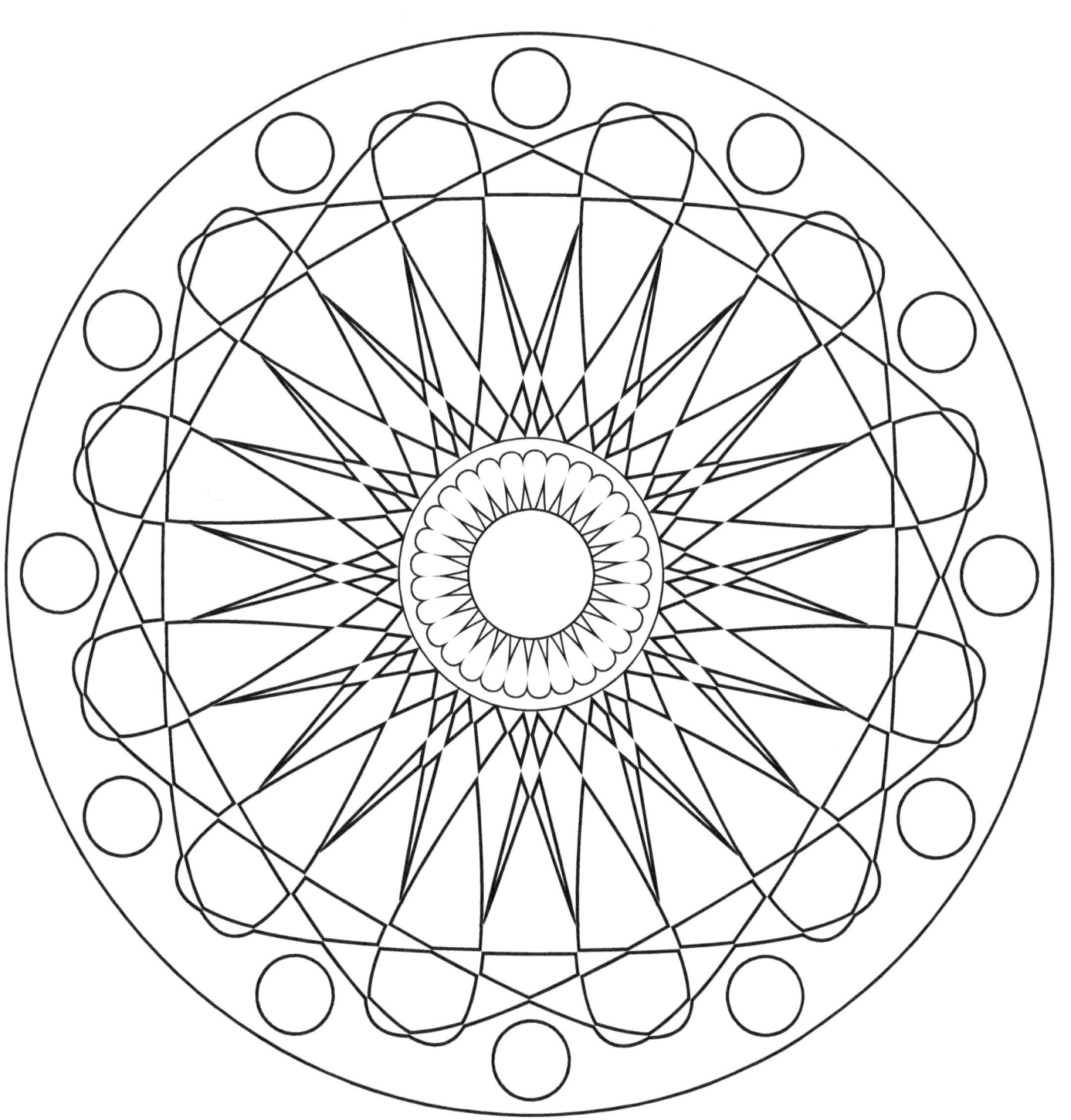

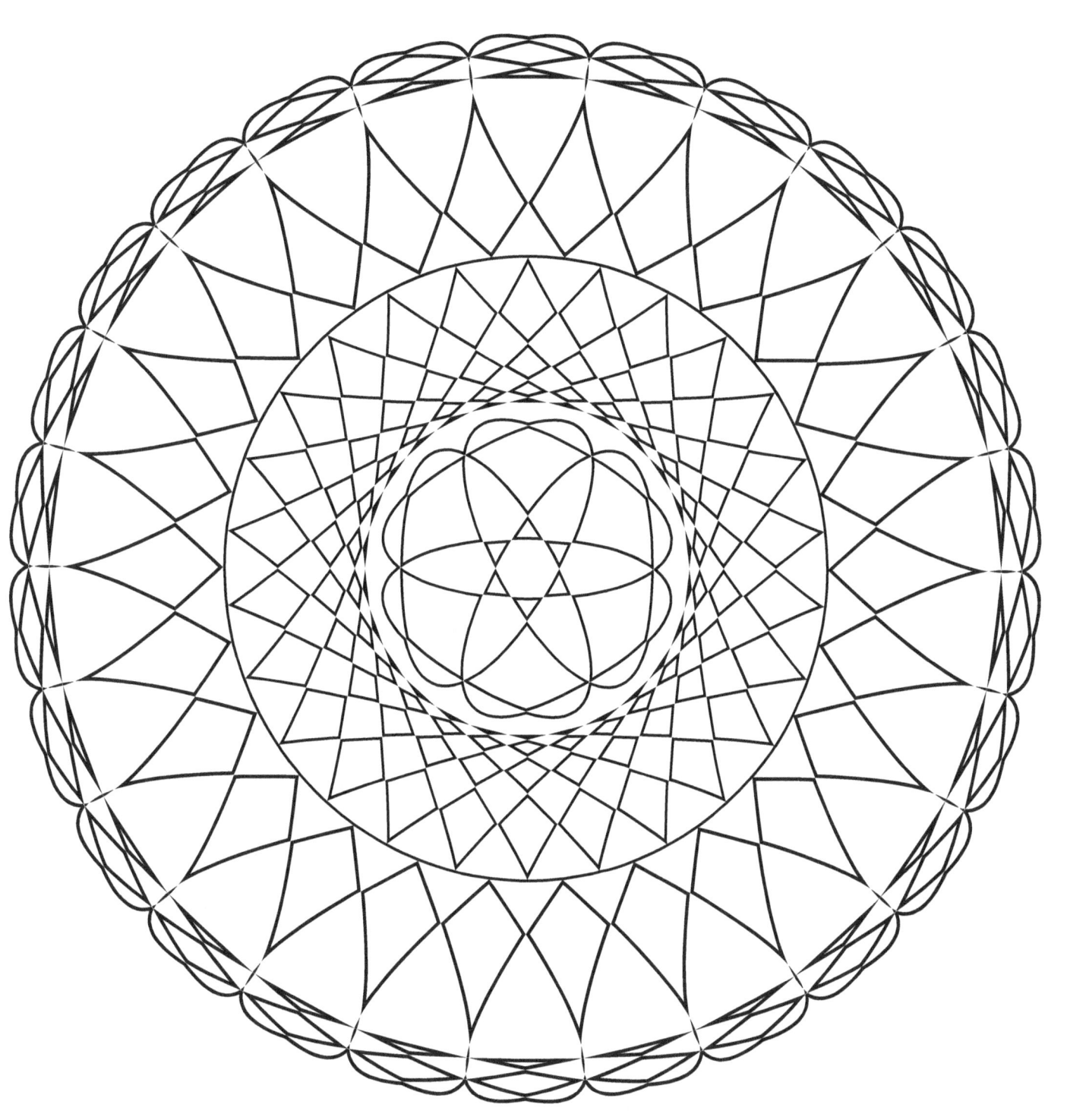

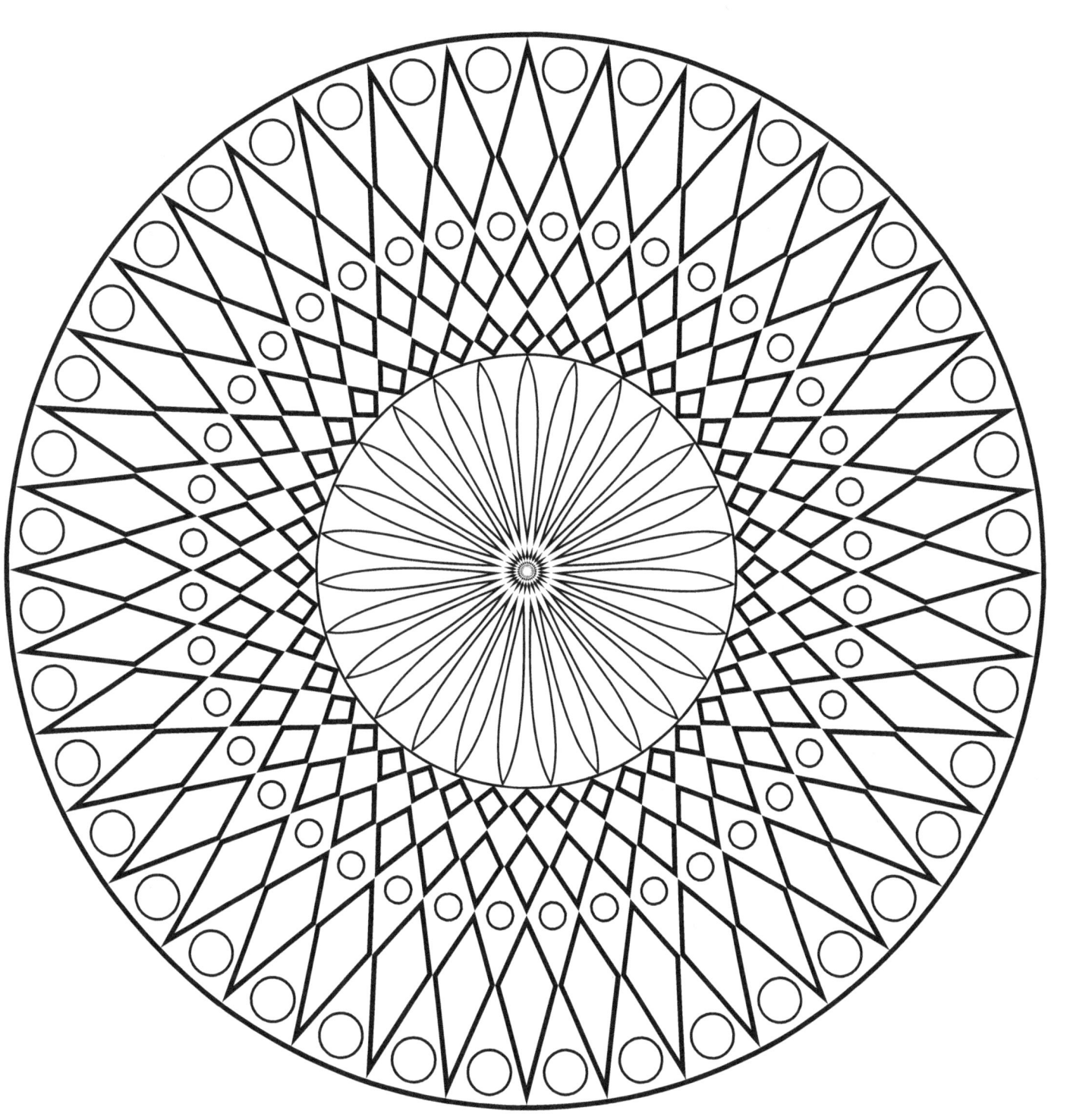

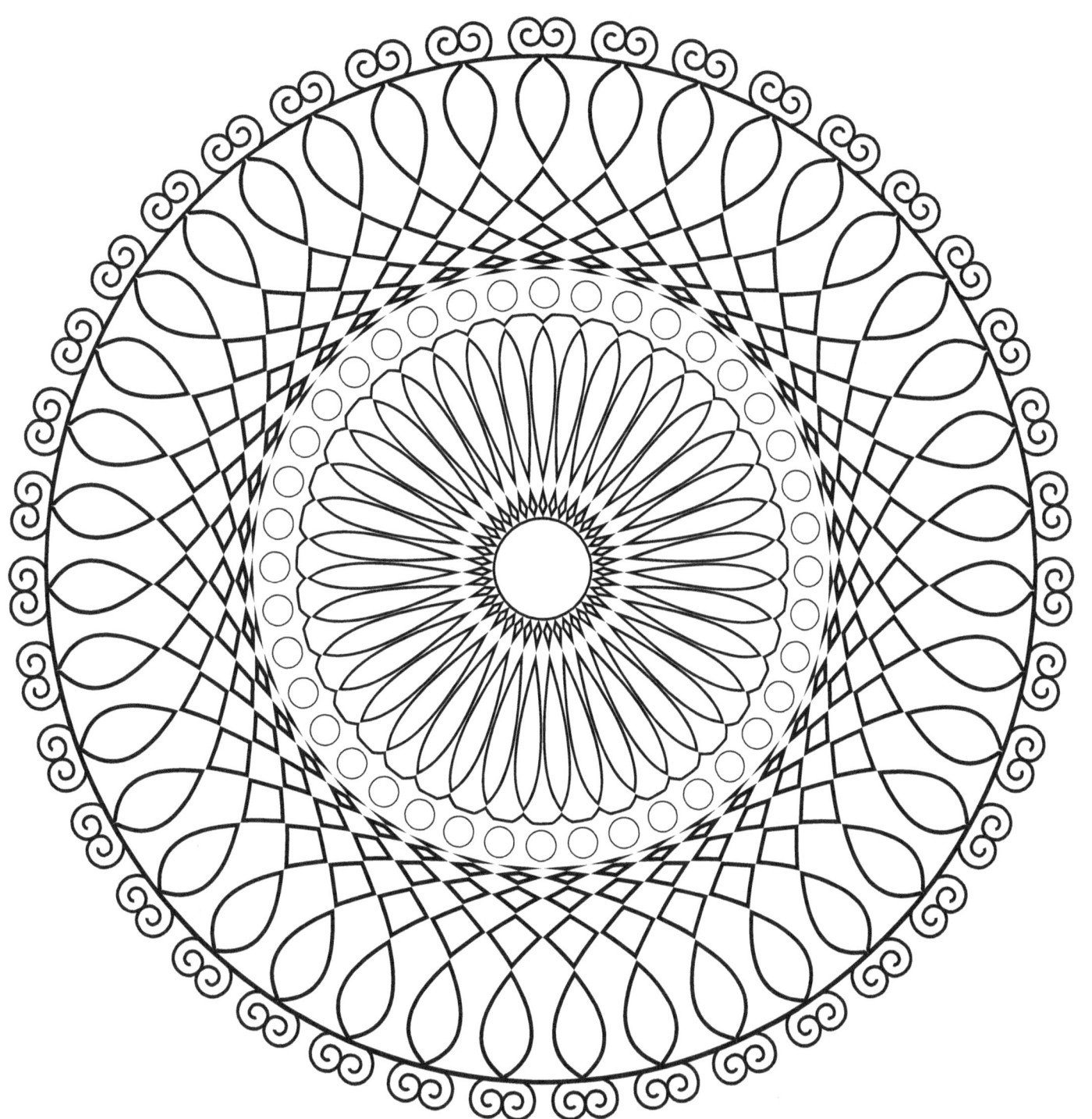

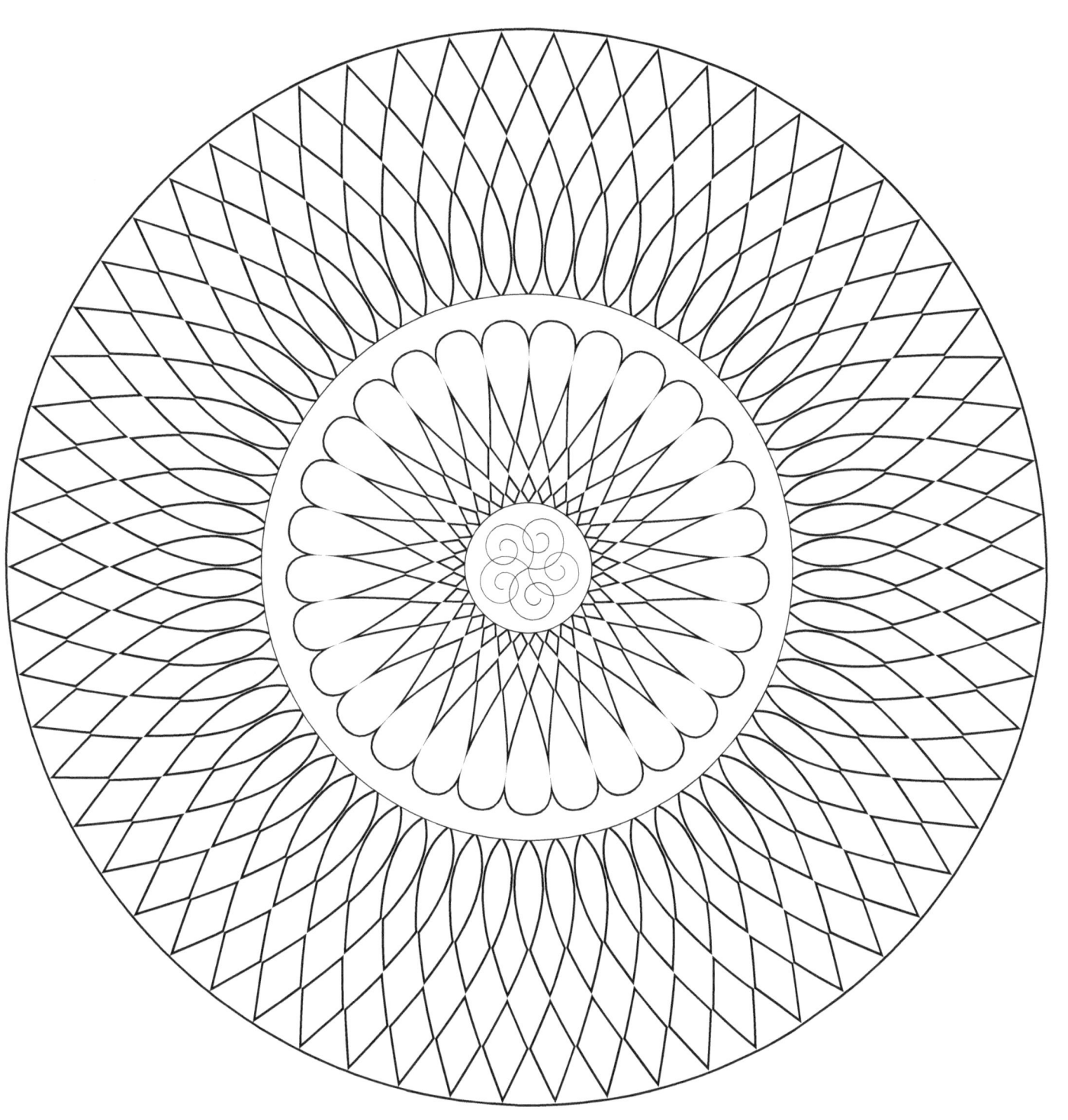

Folgen Sie Modern Studio auf Amazon.
Follow Modern Studio on Amazon.
Sigue a Modern Studio en Amazon.
Segui Modern Studio su Amazon.

https://www.amazon.com/Modern-Studio/e/B0887KDQYG

Instagram, Facebook.

Um über neue Bücher informiert zu werden, senden Sie eine E-Mail an:
To be updated on new books send an email to:
Para estar informado sobre nuevos libros envíe un correo electrónico a:
Per essere aggiornato su nuovi libri invia una mail a:

www.ingramcontent.com/pod-product-compliance
Lightning Source LLC
Chambersburg PA
CBHW081437220526
45466CB00008B/2427